"THE STRAD" LIBRARY, No. XV.

THE
VIOLIN & ITS STORY:
OR THE
HISTORY & CONSTRUCTION
OF THE VIOLIN.

Translated and Adapted from the German of
HYACINTH ABELE
BY
GEOFFREY ALWYN.

WITH TWENTY-EIGHT ILLUSTRATIONS.

1905.

Copyright © 2013 Read Books Ltd.
This book is copyright and may not be
reproduced or copied in any way without
the express permission of the publisher in writing

British Library Cataloguing-in-Publication Data
A catalogue record for this book is available from the
British Library

A History of the Violin

The violin, also known as a fiddle, is a string instrument, usually with four strings tuned in perfect fifths. It is the smallest, highest-pitched member of the violin family of string instruments, which also includes the viola, the cello and the double bass. The violinist produces sound by drawing a bow across one or more strings (which may be stopped by the fingers of the other hand to produce a full range of pitches), by plucking the strings (with either hand), or by a variety of other techniques. The violin is played by musicians in a wide variety of musical genres, including such diverse styles as baroque, classical, jazz, folk and rock and roll.

The violin, while it has ancient origins, acquired most of its modern characteristics in 16th-century Italy, with some further modifications occurring in the 18th and 19th centuries. Violinists and collectors particularly prize the instruments made by the Gasparo da Salò, Giovanni Paolo Maggini, Stradivari, Guarneri and Amati families from the 16th to the 18th century in Brescia and Cremona and by Jacob Stainer in Austria. A person who makes or repairs violins is called a luthier, and will almost always work with wood – utilising gut, perlon or steel to string the instrument.

The history of the violin is long and varied; and the earliest stringed instruments were mostly plucked (e.g. the Greek lyre). Bowed instruments may have originated in the equestrian cultures of Central Asia – for instance the 'Tanbur' of Uzbekistan or the 'Kobyz'; an ancient Turkic string instrument. Such two-string upright fiddles were strung with horsehair and played with horsehair bows; they often features a carved horses head at the end of the neck too. The violins, violas and cellos we play today, and whose bows are still strung with horsehair are a legacy of these nomadic peoples.

It is believed that these instruments eventually spread to China, India, the Byzantine Empire and the Middle East, where they developed into instruments such as the erhu in China, the rebab in the Middle East, the lyra in the Byzantine Empire and the esraj in India. The modern European violin as we know it evolved from the Middle Eastern stringed instruments, and one of the earliest explicit descriptions of this musical device, including its tuning was made in France in the sixteenth century. This was a book entitled *Epitome Musical,* by Jambe de Fer, published in Lyon in 1556 – and helped popularise the instrument all over Europe. Several further significant changes occurred in violin construction in the eighteenth century – making it closer to our current instrument. These primarily involved a longer neck at a slightly different angle, as well as a heavier bass bar.

The oldest documented violin to have four strings, like the modern variant, is supposed to have been constructed in 1555 by Andrea Amati. However in the 1510s (some fifty years before the flourishing activity of Andrea Amati), there were sevedn 'lireri', or makers of bowed instruments, including proto-violins listed in the city. The violin was quickly hailed by nobility and street players alike, illustrated by the fact that the French king Charles IX ordered Amati to construct twenty-four violins for him in 1560. One of these instruments, now called the *Charles IX,* is the oldest surviving violin. The *finest* Renaissance carved and decorated violin in the world is the Gasparo da Salò (c. 1574), owned by Ferdinand II, Archduke of Austria and later, from 1841, by the Norweigian virtuoso Ole Bull. Bull used it for forty years, during which he became famed for his powerful and beautiful tone – it is now kept in the Vestlandske Kustindustrimuseum in Begen (Norway). Another famous violin, 'Le Messie' (also known as the 'Salabue'), made in 1716 is now located in the Ashmolean Museum of Oxford, England.

To this day, instruments from the so-called Golden Age of violin making, especially those made by Stradivari, Guarneri del Gesù and Montagnana are the most sought-after instruments by both collectors and performers. The current record amount paid for a Stradivari violin is £9.8 million (US$15.9 million), when the instrument known as the Lady Blunt was sold by Tarisio Auctions in an online auction on June 20, 2011. We hope the reader is inspired by this book to find out more about the intriguing and complex history of this wonderful instrument.

FOREWORD BY THE TRANSLATOR.

THE devotees of the violin are to be found all over the globe; their name is legion, and their devotion to their fascinating instrument has no parallel in the world of music. Every scrap of information about the origin, the history, or the development of the string family, and above all, about the violin itself, is gratefully accepted and eagerly read and re-read by its hundreds of thousands of worshippers, who regard their "fiddles" with a loving enthusiasm which is felt for no other instrument in the whole realm of musical art. The translator feels, therefore, that no apology is needed for introducing to violin lovers the following chapters of a work which he has himself read with intense pleasure, and the ranslation o which into his mother tongue has been to him a veritable "labour of love"; because he is certain at the outset that the reading of what he has translated with so much enjoyment will afford the readers of this volume a like gratification.

In turning Abele's work into English, I have here and there put a note to remind the reader that his book was written about forty years ago. This must be constantly remembered in reading this work; and the reader will easily be able to understand how Abele would have treated his subject if he had written at the end of the nineteenth century. The book has long been out of print, and cannot be bought even in Germany. Its contents, however, are of such great value—and show so much original research, as well as great artistic insight and a lively appreciation of the subject on which the author writes—that this English translation will, without doubt, afford much gratification to all interested in the violin.

G. A.

CONTENTS.

PART I.

PAGE

THE MOST ANCIENT FORM OF BOWED INSTRUMENTS: THE RAVANASTRON, THE REBEK, THE CROUTH. INTRODUCTION OF THE REBEK INTO WESTERN EUROPE BY THE ARABS. THE GRADUAL DEVELOPMENT OF THE REBEK FROM THE TENTH TO THE FIFTEENTH CENTURY. CONDITION OF INSTRUMENTAL MUSIC IN THE MIDDLE AGES. SIXTEENTH CENTURY AUTHORS ON MUSIC—VIRDUNG, JUDENKÜNIG, ETC. PRÆTORIUS ON STRINGED INSTRUMENTS AT THE BEGINNING OF THE SIXTEENTH CENTURY 1

PART II.

THE OLDEST MASTERS OF THE ART OF THE LUTE-MAKER: JOAN KERLINO, 1449; PIETRO DARDELLI, 1500; KASPAR DUIFFOPRUGAR, 1510; ETC., ETC. SCHOOL OF BRESCIA—THE FIRST VIOLIN MAKERS, GASPAR DA SALO, J. P. MAGGINI, ETC. SCHOOL OF CREMONA—THE AMATI, ANT. STRADIVARIO (STRADIVARIUS), GIUSEPPE GUARNERIO (GUARNERIUS). PUPILS OF THESE MASTERS. THE SCHOOLS OF MILAN, VENICE, ETC. THE GERMAN SCHOOL: JACOBUS STAINER, ALBANI, M. KLOTZ, ETC. FOUNDING OF THE ART AT MITTENWALD. GERMAN MASTERS WHO FOLLOWED THE ITALIANS, OR COPIED STAINER. FRENCH MASTERS: LUPOT, GAND, VUILLAUME. THE FORTUNES OF THE ART OF VIOLIN MAKING, FROM STAINER TO THE PRESENT TIME. THE EXPERIMENTS OF THE VARIOUS MASTERS; SAVART'S INVESTIGATIONS. THE DECLINE OF THE VIOLIN MAKER'S ART, AND ITS CAUSES. 34

PART III.

THE CHIEF CONSTITUENT PARTS OF THE VIOLIN. 1.—*The Strings.* VIBRATION, FLEXIBILITY, WEIGHT, LENGTH, ELASTICITY, HARMONICS. TARTINI'S COMBINATION-TONES. CONDITIONS OF PITCH, STRENGTH, AND QUALITY OF TONE. GUT-STRING MANUFACTURE IN ITALY AND GERMANY. PRACTICAL HINTS. 2. *The Tone-producing body.* THE CONDITIONS UNDER WHICH THE TONE IS STRENGTHENED, NOT ONLY BY THE VIBRATIONS OF AIR, BUT BY THE VIBRATIONS OF THE WOOD ITSELF. MOLECULAR VIBRATION OF BELLY AND BACK. PRACTICAL ADVICE FOR SELECTING THE BEST MATERIALS FOR BELLY, BACK, AND SIDES. THE DIVISIONS OF THICKNESS OF WOOD FOR BELLY AND BACK. ANTON BAGATELLA'S RULES. 3. *Bass-bar, Sound-post, and Bridge.* THE GRADUAL PERFECTION OF BASS-BAR AND BRIDGE. THE NECK, THE FINGER-BOARD, THE NUT, THE TAILPIECE, THE VARNISH. THE BOW AND ITS GRADUAL DEVELOPMENT, UP TO THE HIGHEST FORM BY TOURTE. CONCLUDING REMARKS. 77

LIST OF ILLUSTRATIONS.

	PAGE
FRONTISPIECE: JOSEPH GUARNERIUS VIOLIN.	
TITLE PAGE: MEDIÆVAL FIDDLERS.	
RAVANASTRON	4
OMERTI	5
REBEK (ANCIENT)	6
CROUTH—THREE-STRINGED	8
CROUTH—SIX-STRINGED	11
REBEK	13
REBEK, FROM NOTKER'S "PSALM BOOK"	13
VIOLIN OF THIRTEENTH CENTURY	15
VIRDUNG'S "GREAT FIDDLE"	22
,, "LITTLE FIDDLE"	24
ANCIENT PRINT FROM HANS JUDENKUNIG	28
TENOR GAMBA	30
FORERUNNERS OF THE VIOLIN	32
VIBRATIONS OF STRINGS	79
HARMONICS	83
COMBINATION TONES	84
TESTING STRINGS	92
BAGATELLA'S MODEL	101
BRIDGE FROM SEVEN-STRINGED VIOL	107
,, ,, FIVE-STRINGED VIOL	107
,, ,, ANTON AMATI VIOLIN	108
,, ,, NICHOLAS AMATI VIOLIN	108
STRADIVARIUS'S BRIDGE	109
PROPER CURVE OF BRIDGE	111
SPOHR'S FINGER-BOARD	111
EVOLUTION OF THE BOW	113

The Violin and its Story.

PART I.

The most ancient form of bowed instruments : the Ravanastron, the Omerti, the Rebek, the Crouth. Introduction of the Rebek into western Europe by the Arabs. The gradual development of the Rebek from the tenth to the fifteenth century. Condition of Instrumental Music in the Middle Ages. Sixteenth century authors on music—Virdung, Judenkünig, etc. Prætorius on Stringed Instruments at the beginning of the sixteenth century.

It is usual to divide musical instruments into four chief classes, according to the method of their construction and the manner in which they are played. These classes are respectively named Stringed Instruments, Keyboard Instruments, Wind Instruments, and Instruments of Percussion. The group of stringed instruments is again divided into those in which the strings are plucked, and those in which the strings are played by a bow; and the purpose of the following pages is to set forth the history and construction of the chief of the latter class, viz., THE VIOLIN. It is not without good reason that we confine our attention exclusively to the violin as the chief of the whole class of stringed instruments. For, in the first place, the class of plucked or pulled string instruments, such as the guitar and lute, being of so much less importance than the fiddle, whether as regards their construction or their place in the orchestra, they cannot be treated as at all in the same category as the latter;

B

and in the second place it is hardly necessary to deal separately with the other bowed instruments—the Viola, the 'Cello, and the Double Bass, which with the violin constitute the foundation of the orchestra, seeing that they only differ from the violin in size, and not necessarily in form, while the principles on which they are built are precisely the same as those which govern the construction of the violin.

The primordial savage was wont to stretch a piece of dried gut over a big shell or hollowed-out calabash for a "sound-box," or to fasten a piece of similar gut to the end of a bent stick, one end of which he would put in his mouth while he twanged the string with his finger, thus making a sound out of which it must be supposed he got a little "musical" enjoyment. What a vast gulf between these primitive attempts and the perfect violins of the Cremonese artists Stradivarius and Guarnerius! And yet it is with these self-same primitive efforts that the long history of the construction of stringed instruments must begin. Between these attempts, totally lacking in knowledge of science or of art, and the perfect works of the master artificers of the violin, there stretches a wide chasm, and the materials for filling up that chasm are but scant. If we attempt, from such sources as are available, to fill it up to some extent, the reader must be left to decide how far success has rewarded our efforts.

To arrive at any conclusion on the question of the genesis of bowed instruments, it will be necessary to give some attention to the cultivated peoples of bygone ages. It is the custom nowadays to speak of the Greeks and Romans as having possessed no instruments similar to our own stringed instruments, although a belief in the existence of the Mágadis has long been held.* This Mágadis was fitted with twenty strings tuned in octaves. J. B. Doni says it resembled the "Viola di Bordune," which was also called the "Lirone," which was in use in Italy in the sixteenth century, was fitted with eleven or twelve strings, and on which *arpeggi* were played with

---

* Mágadis, a harp of twenty strings.

the bow. Such conjectures possess, however, no historical value, for in the old writers no trace can be found of the Greeks using any instrument which could be likened to our own stringed instruments. Attempts have been made to find in the "plectrum" the origin of our wooden bow, and, indeed some dictionaries give the meaning of "plectrum" as "the bow of a musical instrument"; but this betrays a confusion of ideas as to the true meanings of words. Greek statues and bas-reliefs, as also the paintings upon their pottery, give us plenty of representations of the "plectrum," but it is easily discerned to be a little piece of wood or ivory held in the hand of the player, fitted with a hook, with which he gripped or struck the strings. Greek and Roman sculpture and painting show us no single example of anything at all resembling a bow.

On the other hand, India would appear to have been the cradle of stringed instruments, and it is now generally accepted that these were brought over originally from Asia to Europe. It is also known that India contains the most ancient monuments of a very advanced civilisation, and it is certain that the inhabitants of that land have for thousands of years maintained the *status quo* of their peculiar culture. Precisely on these grounds the musical instruments there discovered establish their character of primitive originality, and the simplicity of contrivance shown in those instruments leaves no doubt possible as to the origin of bowed instruments. Fétis gives an interesting description of the "Ravanastron," the oldest and most widely used instrument of its species in India, somewhat as follows:—

The Ravanastron consists of a hollow box or cup of sycamore wood, eleven centimetres long and five centimetres wide. Upon one side of this box is stretched a piece of broad-scaled boa-skin, the position of which causes it to act as a sound-board or resonance table. To one end of the box is fixed a piece of wood fifty-five centimetres long, bored at its upper end with two holes. This piece of wood serves as the neck of the instrument, the two strings being fastened to pegs fitted into the two holes at the end of the neck. On the under side of this neck is fastened a strip of serpent skin which serves as a holder. The bridge is eighteen millimetres in length, slanting on the upper side, and cut out below in rectangular fashion so as to make two feet. The strings were of gazelle gut. The bow consisted of a light piece of bamboo reed, and in one end of this reed a hollow place was made in which to fasten a bundle of horse hair, which was drawn tight, and fastened at the other end by a very flexible braided reed tightly wound round it. Thus far Fétis.

The Indians as a people, unlike the Chinese, do not like noisy music, and the tone of the Ravanastron (Fig. 1)

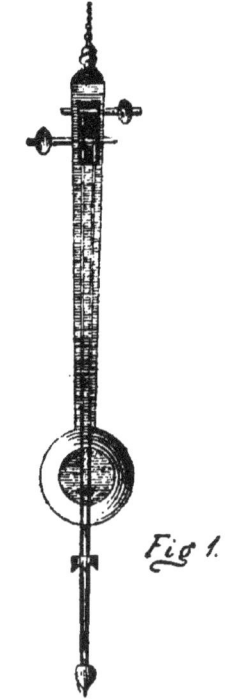

THE RAVANASTRON.

was weak and dull, though pleasant. According to Indian tradition, this instrument was invented by Ravana, who was king of Ceylon 5,000 years before the Christian era, and even at the present day it is found in use by the Panderons, a genus of wandering Buddhist monks; while the poorer class of Indians use an instrument somewhat differing from the Ravanastron, but resembling it in its general features.

The Omerti (Fig. 2) is in its construction brought to a

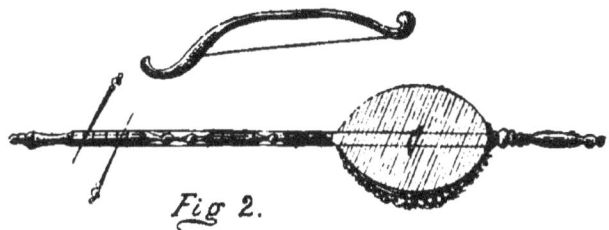

THE OMERTI.

higher finish than the Ravanastron, but is also a two-stringed bowed instrument. The body consists of a cocoa-nut shell, of which one-third is cut away, and the remaining part reduced to a thickness of two millimetres. The sound-table is sometimes of wood, and sometimes of the skin of an animal, while the bridge resembles that of the Ravanastron.

The two instruments just mentioned cannot, it is self-evident, be considered to be in the realm of art, but must be classed as producers of the original folks-music. Other oriental instruments may be included in the same category—instruments built on similar lines to the Ravanastron and the Omerti, their differences in form being traceable solely to the fancy of their makers. To this class belongs the Rebab (Rebeb, Erbeb, or Rebek) (Fig. 3) of the Arabs. The body of this instrument consists of thin strips, slabs, or ribs of wood of a wedge-like form, across which are stretched two pieces of parchment to form what may be called the "back" and "belly" of the Rebek. The finger-board is cylindrical in form, and it and the head are made from one piece of wood. The foot consists of a rod of iron, which goes through the interior of the body, and is fastened to the lower end of the finger-board. The instrument, while it is being played, rests on this foot. The Rebab had only one string, and was entirely used to accompany one or more voices.

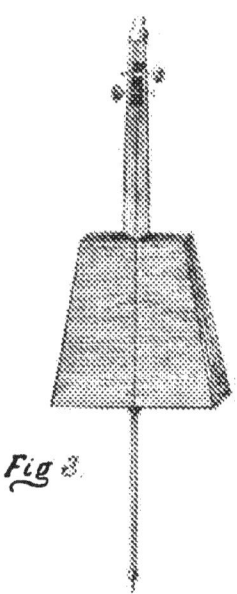

THE REBEK, OR REBAB.

While it is not our purpose to give further instances of instruments of the above class, it is at the same time to be remarked that in the writings on music which have come down to us from ancient oriental nations, we do not always find perfect agreement amongst them as to the descriptions or sketches of the instruments depicted in Figures 1, 2, 3. This, however, is not of any great importance, as it is sufficient for our purpose to demonstrate in what direction the story of the origin of bowed instruments is to be looked for. A more important matter is—When did stringed instruments played with the bow come into use in the west?

Before the end of the eighth or the beginning of the ninth century no trace is to be found of the existence of stringed instruments on the continent of Europe, but a poet named Venans Fortunat, Bishop of Poitiers, who died about A.D. 609, and who is said to have written some elegant poems about the year 570, tells us that the Crwth or Crouth of the Welsh Bards was known in his day, and that it was probably known in England before his own time. In the following verse the poet spells the word as " chrotta " :—

" Romanusque lyra plaudat tibi, Barbara harpa,
Græcus achilliaca, *chrotta* Brittanna canat."

which may be vernacularised thus :—

"The Romans praised thee upon the lyre, the Barbarian with the harp;
The Greeks with the cither, and the Britons with the *crouth*."

About the middle of the fifth century, as is well known, the Saxons conquered a part of England, and it may be thought that they brought the Crouth with them. But this idea, plausible as it is at first sight, will not hold water when we remember that the Welsh were never subdued by the Saxons; that the Crouth remained for a long time unknown to any other people than the Welsh in these islands: and that later on its use was restricted almost entirely to Wales. The researches of our *savans* have proved beyond doubt that the Welsh people are of Indo-Germanic descent, and we have no grounds for believing otherwise than that the original home of the Crouth was India. That the Crouth was improved in the course of the centuries, is evident from some of the pictures of it which have come down to our own day.

The most ancient form of this instrument is the " Crouth trithant," that is, the crouth with three strings, which is probably the one of which Venans Fortunat spoke. A MS. of the eleventh century, which came originally from the Abbey of St. Martial at Limoges,

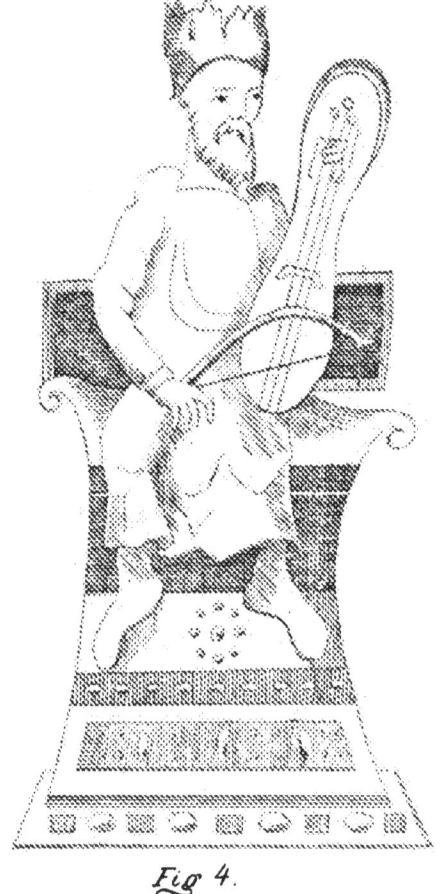

Fig 4.

"Three-stringed Crouth."

and a Latin version of which is in the Imperial Library at Paris, No. 1118, contains drawings of somewhat ungainly figures holding instruments, and amongst them a crowned person holding in his left hand a three-stringed Crouth, and in his right hand a bow. Fig. 4 is a reproduction of this figure.

The instrument is recognised by the opening through which the left hand is pushed so that it may finger the strings. Another representation of the " Crouth trithant " is to be found amongst the architectural embellishments of Melrose Abbey, in Scotland, which was built in the early years of the fourteenth century.

How long the three-stringed Crouth maintained its ground is difficult to say, as we can trace no references to the instrument until well on into the eighteenth century, when we find the Crouth in a very advanced state, and fitted with six strings. Daines Barrington, a magistrate in the Welsh counties of Anglesey and Carnarvon, knew a bard named John Morgan, born in the Island of Anglesey in 1711, who played upon a six-stringed Crouth. Morgan played this instrument before Barrington, who made a good drawing of it, which he published, with some comments, in a work on archæology. This description of the Crouth, together with some further information furnished by one Edward Jones, enabled Fétis to give the following particulars of the instrument:—

The Crouth is in the shape of an elongated trapezoid, having a length, from top to base, of fifty-seven centimetres; its greatest width, at the tailpiece, is twenty-seven centimetres; its narrowest part, at the upper end, is twenty-three centimetres in width; and its thickness at the edges five centimetres. The finger-board is twenty-eight centimetres long. Of the six strings with which the Crouth is fitted, two lie outside the finger-board, and are merely plucked with the thumb of the left hand. The other four strings are played with the bow. At the lower end the strings are held by the tailpiece, while at the upper end they go through holes bored in the frame; the strings rest on a ridge, and are held by pegs on the under side of the instrument, which pegs are turned by a key or lever. The table has two circular sound-holes, of a diameter of three centimetres. There is one feature about the bridge of the Crouth which is of great interest to the intelligent observer, viz., its peculiar position and the unequal height of its feet. The right end of the bridge is nearer the tailpiece than the left end; the left foot is about seven centimetres long, goes through the left sound-hole, and rests on the back of the instrument; the right foot, on the other hand, resting on the table or belly, near the right sound hole, is only two centimetres high. It will therefore be seen that the left foot of the bridge serves a similar purpose to that of the sound-post of the violin.

Fig. 5 shows the drawing given by the above-mentioned Edward Jones, which clearly shows the position of the left foot of the bridge.

The tuning of the Crouth was as follows:—

That this method of tuning was not universal, however, is shown by a statement made by Mr. Bingley in 1801, who heard a Crouth player at Carnarvon who tuned his instrument thus:—

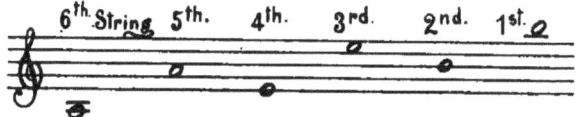

The reader will gather, from the details of the Crouth here given, that to manufacture this instrument required the highest skill of the lute-maker, and further, that the Crouth received all the improvements of which its construction was capable. We have already stated that its use in certain parts of England gradually diminished; and it is certain that the Crouth exercised no influence on the development of the violin itself, for the opinion is generally accepted, and may be maintained on clear

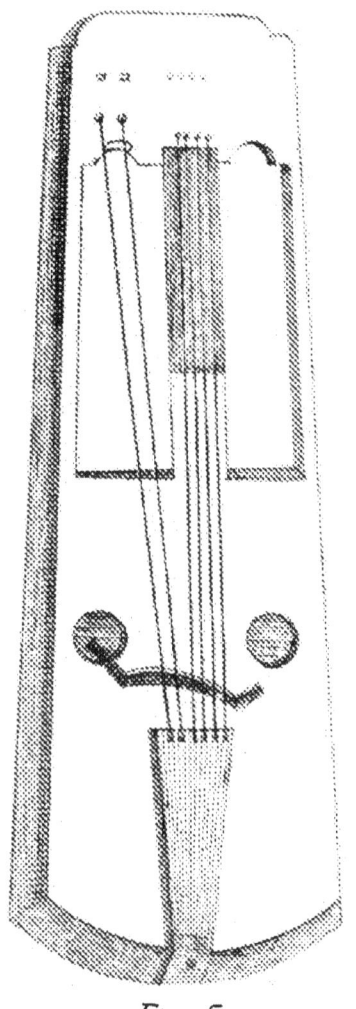

Fig 5.

THE CROUTH.

grounds, that the latter is traceable to the Rebab or Rebek of the Arabs.

When we endeavour to trace the development of bowed instruments from the Carolingian era, we find very little help from the few remaining adventitious samples of the plastic and draughtsman's arts. In the thirteenth century the learned musicians, writers, and poets take no notice of the class of instruments in question. The passage in Ottfried's "Evengelienharmonie," is the single exception known to us:—

"Sih thas ouh al ruarit, thaz organa fuarit
lira, ioh fidula, ioh managfaltu suegula,"

(There moved all those who carried instruments,
The lyre and *fiedel* and many sorts of pipes.)

Here appears for the first time the name of "Fiedel." It is difficult to understand why many will not see in Ottfried's "fidula" a stringed instrument, but merely the "fidicula" of the ancients.

The oldest representation of the Rebek is found in a manuscript of Abbot Gerbert of the ninth century. (See Fig. 6). In this picture it has only one string, the half-moon-shaped sound-holes are cut in the table, and the string passes over the bridge. One part of the handle, or neck, appears to stand higher than the table.

In the next century the Rebek is shown with two, sometimes three, strings. If the painter or sculptor occasionally shows it with four strings, it results either from carelessness or ignorance. The same instrument is at one time shown with a bow, and at another without one; now under one name, and then under another. It is quite useless to expect any exactitude in the real sense of the word.

Notker's* Psalm Book (tenth century) contains a picture of a Rebek with a bow, as in Fig. 7.

---

* Notker was a monk of St. Galle, and died in 1022. In poetical and musical gifts he surpassed all his contemporaries. Many of his poems attained great fame, and the common people, impressed by the power of his verse, maintained that he gave the devil such a sound drubbing with a hazel rod that his Satanic majesty endowed him with the poetic gift.

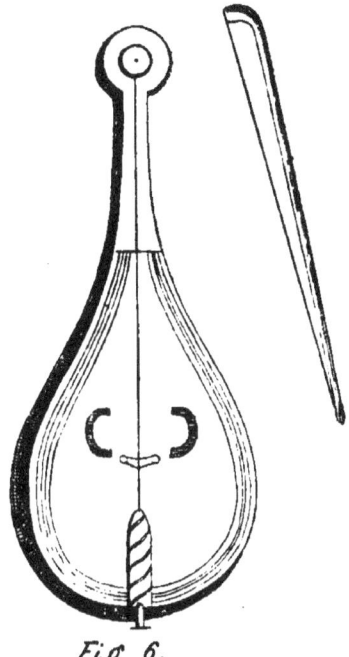

Fig 6.
THE REBEK.

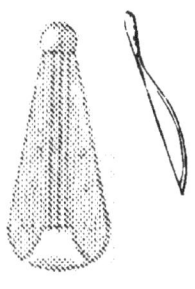

Fig 7.
REBEK (from Notker's Psalm Book).

Two pen and ink drawings, which stand as ornaments at the beginning of Notker's book, represent King David sitting on his throne, and playing a seven-stringed lyre with a plectrum. In each of the four corners of the page is a figure, one playing on the violin (Rebek), a second on the cither, a third on the dulcimer, and a fourth on the harp. From the scrupulous care with which these fine drawings are made, it is evident that the artist did not invent or draw upon his imagination, but had examples before his eyes.

From the eleventh century onwards pictures of bowed instruments are more plentiful.

In the Church of St. Michael at Pavia, the oldest portion of which dates from the sixth century, there is a representation in relief, of the eleventh century, of a player with a bowed instrument.

On the capital of St. George's Church, Bocherville, also of the eleventh century, is sculptured a row of eleven musical figures. There we see a three-stringed viol, with an inlet on each side, and four halfmoon-shaped sound-holes, the player holding the instrument between his knees; and also a four-stringed elliptical "arm-fiddle," which the eighth musician, a crowned figure seated, plays in the usual way.

Prior to the French Revolution, there was to be seen at Nôtre Dame, Paris, at the right hand entrance under the dome, a crowned, standing figure, which Montfaucon believed was intended for King Chilperic. The figure held an instrument fitted with four strings, elegantly cut, and the instrument much narrowed round the neck. The table was flat and continued right up to the neck. This statue belonged to the eleventh century, and was transferred from the old church to the new.

In the interior of the Abbey of St. Germain des Près, Paris, probably of the twelfth century, is a bearded man carved in stone, who holds in his left hand a large five-stringed viol, which he is playing with a bow held in his right hand. The body of the instrument is long and elliptical, without inlets, and with two long sound-holes, bent inwards, above the bridge. The edge is ornamented with inlaid ivory or mother-of-pearl.

Three figures over the portal of the Abbey of St. Denis, built in the twelfth century, hold " violins " with three or five strings; while the Cathedral of Nôtre Dame at Chartres, of the same century, has amongst its sculptures a fiddle with three strings, but with nothing resembling a bridge.

In Fig. 8 we have a representation of a violin which forms the vignette of a MS. to be seen at Paris, and which appears to belong to the thirteenth century. This

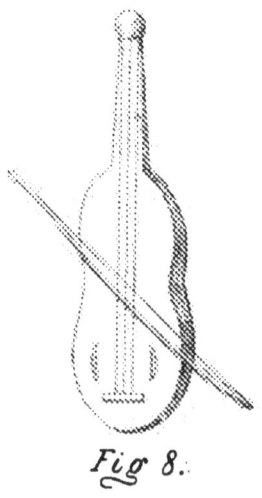

Fig 8.

instrument approaches more nearly to the present form of the violin, the edges having two gentle bends inwards, suggesting the middle bouts of our violin, and the " F holes " are represented by two halfmoon-shaped openings, turning towards each other. The bow, however, differs but little from that in Notker's Psalm Book.

In the museum at Prague is preserved a parchment manuscript, written between 1202 and 1212, and known under the name of "Mater Verborum." Amongst the miniature paintings, which are unusually beautiful and artistic for that period, is an angel holding a fiddle in its hand. In another parchment manuscript, the Bible of Jaromèr, dating from 1529, there are several figures holding similar instruments. Another figure holding a three-stringed violin is to be seen in a manuscript of the fourteenth century in the Imperial Library at Paris. It is the figure of a woman seated on a horse, and it is evident that this instrument has a volute somewhat like that of the modern violin. Again, in the Castle of Carlstein, in Bohemia, which was built in the fourteenth century, there is a representation of a bowed instrument which very nearly resembles the violin of to-day—a proof that the art of violin-making must have made great strides from the thirteenth to the fourteenth century.

Besides the above, there are numerous other evidences of the condition and progress of the violin-maker's art. In the meantime it is worthy of remark, that we are almost entirely dependent upon such accidentally preserved relics of the pictorial art as have come down to us, for our ideas of that progress down to the close of the fifteenth century, although among these relics there are undoubtedly some which are to the last degree deceptive. However thankful we are in the habit of feeling for such archæological mile-stones, it must at the same time be matter for great surprise that information from the learned men and the musicians of those days is almost entirely wanting. Even where such information has reached us it is exceedingly meagre, and gives us no glimpse whatever of the knowledge we so much desire as to the condition of bowed instruments or the method of their handling.

Thus Jerome of Moravia, a Dominican friar of the thirteenth century, talking about the Rebek, merely says that the instrument of this name was of a deep tone, and that its two strings were tuned C and G. The writer, also, of an anonymous dissertation on musical instruments, which belong to the thirteenth century, informs us that a certain Albinus invented a viol of four strings which he says were tuned:—

but as to who and what this Albinus was, and where or when he lived, we are left altogether in the dark. It was only in the beginning of the sixteenth century that writers began to give us any reliable information about stringed instruments, and from that period onwards it is much easier to trace out their further development.

It is perhaps not difficult to explain the indifference of mediæval writers to this topic, or their entire silence concerning it. From the earlier centuries of the Christian era until well on into the middle ages, the arts, and all kinds of erudition, were the sole property of the Church and of the cloistered clergy; and the best of the arts, music among the rest, were exclusively employed in the service of the Church; while even here, for the most part, voices only were used, to the exclusion of all instruments, except the organ. Instrumental music,—if one may apply the term to the beginnings of things—rested in those days in the hands of one, or at most two, classes of people, who in France were described as Troubadours, Romancers, Minstrels, and so on. They recited, sang, played, made jests, and travelled about the country in the company of rope-dancers, jugglers, and conjurers. Partly by their wandering lives, and partly by their connection with men whose arts were either noble in themselves, or else served a useful purpose, these "wandering lutists" commanded a vast amount of attention. The Church put them under its ban, and the society of the towns regarded them as outlaws and without any rights. Their children could learn no trade, because they were regarded as of unholy birth; and when these people died, the authorities seized their property. Sought by many, yet pursued by the law, they led the life of vagabonds. These conditions lasted so long as the disorderly and unsettled lives of these people, and their mixing up of noble and base arts, endured; but the enlightenment of the age, and the constantly growing requirements of a generally improving taste, conduced in progress of time to a vast improvement in the condition of these banned wandering musicians. When their arts came to be looked upon with less favour, they found it absolutely necessary to seek more lasting dwelling places; a more settled state of life led to a more extended development of their musical powers; and this development led, in the long run, to a complete separation of such of their arts as were capable of nobler things from the jugglery and other tricks which had, from the very nature of their former mode of life, been mixed up with music, but with which those tricks had no natural connection. From these hitherto despised wandering minstrels, who had in past times been universally condemned by the law, players upon all sorts of instruments were selected for public processions, dances, and festivals, and finally they were employed even in the services of the Church. Thus did these "wandering musicians," who had once been despised and condemned by the public authorities, became at length orderly and useful members of the body politic.

In the meantime we find that the handling of musical instruments was not entirely confined to the class known as "vagrant minstrels." The playing of musical instruments had been adopted by some who were under no necessity whatever to play them as a means of livelihood. As early as the beginning of the thirteenth century, it was regarded as no dishonourable thing to play an instrument for people to dance to. This is shown by a passage in the Brunswick chronicles for the year 1203, which relate that at Whitsuntide in that year, at Ossemer near Stendal, while the parish priest was "fiddling at a dance," a fearful storm came on, the right arm of the reverend "fiddler" was struck off by lightning, and twenty-four people were killed.*

But the surest proof that at this period the art of handling the fiddle and the bow was held in great repute, is to be found in our great national epic,† the "Nibelungenlied," which originated about 1210. The poet here describes one of his noblest characters in the bold and jovial Volker of Alzei, who used the sword as freely as he used the fiddle-bow. In this poem Gunther tells Hagen that "the tones of the player resounded through the hall," and that "his fiddle-bow was of red steel." He then calls the king's attention to the beauty of the music, which he says is worth all the king's silver and gold; and, says he, "his fiddle-bow pierces through steel and iron when it falls on helmet and shield."

The forming of an orchestra, which reliable published accounts show to have originated about the beginning of this same thirteenth century, is traceable from a passage in Ulrich of Lichtenstein's "Frauendienst." When Ulrich, in the spring of 1228, undertook his adventurous journey to the Neuburg Tournament, he had in his train two mounted players on the sackbut, a "flute-blower" who also played a drum,‡ and "two fiddlers," who, Ulrich tells us, "played a merry walking tune," *i.e.*, a "march."

In the times of the Minnesingers music fell on better days. The players upon instruments had then ample

---

* This old chronicle is quoted by Abele to show that respectable people, as well as wandering vagabonds and minstrels, played on musical instruments. The event was probably recorded by the Brunswickers themselves as a signal mark of the judgments of heaven falling on the frocked fiddler for encouraging dancing and such like levities.—*Translator.*

† That is, the great epic of the German people.—*Translator.*

‡ This flute-blower perhaps played the "Pan's pipes" and played his drum at the same time, as we remember in our youthful days the proprietor of the Punch and Judy show used to do to gather a crowd round him. He always stuck his pipes into his waistcoat, moved his head round according to the pipes he wished to blow into, and tootled while he drummed, he being the entire "band" of the establishment.—*Translator.*

opportunities of exhibiting their powers, as in summer they were in great demand for tournaments, in winter for assemblies of ladies, dances, and other merrymakings; even the songs sung at these gatherings were accompanied by instruments, while the dancers footed it around at the same time. These blithe wandering players for a long period held sway at the tournaments, as well as at the feasts in the halls of the nobles, while dry and learned musicians laboured heavily on in the footsteps of Hucbald, Guido, and Franco of Cologne.

It would appear that musicians formed themselves into corporate guilds much earlier in France than in Germany. Philip the Magnificent, as early as 1235, elevated to the rank of " Roi de Ribauds " one Charmilion, of the town of Troyes, " on account of his talents in violin-playing." In Paris, in 1330, a society was constituted by the name of the " Brothers of St. Julien of the Minstrels "; and on the 23rd of November in that same year, by which time they were established on a proper footing, they selected St. Genest, a Roman juggler, who was converted to Christianity and suffered martyrdom under Diocletian, as their patron saint and presiding genius under the title of " King of the Minstrels." The entire brotherhood dwelt in one street, which was called after them the " Street of St. Julien of the Minstrels." A later president of this Brotherhood styled himself " King of the Fiddlers." The Brotherhood would seem to have been filled with an unquenchable desire to extend their powers, and in later days sought to bring organists, and even dancing-masters, under their control and domination. This overweening greed of power led ultimately to their downfall, though it was not until 1773 that this powerful guild was at length disbanded by the King's command.

In Germany similar guilds were formed, some of which have survived to modern days. There existed certain high officials who controlled all sports and amusements, and whose jurisdiction extended not only over the largest towns, but sometimes over entire provinces. The powers of these officials were bestowed upon them by the King, and in earlier times they were always selected from the nobility.

These two epochs of instrumental music—viz., that of the wandering minstrels, and that later time in which the growing importance of the great towns served to develop the incorporation of bodies or guilds of musicians—afford very little information that serves our present purpose. The real progress of the art of playing upon stringed instruments cannot be traced with much certainty until the sixteenth century, but from that time forward more reliable historical information is at our disposal. In early days, and more particularly in the beginning of the history of stringed instruments, it is quite possible that the men who used these instruments made them for themselves; but from the early part of the sixteenth century, the engravings of instruments to be found in old works prove that their construction called for well and carefully trained artificers. A few extracts from some of these old works, which are so scarce that they are not likely to be in the hands of the general reader, will be apposite to our present purpose.

The oldest book on the subject with which we are dealing is the "Musika getutscht" (German music) of Sebastian Virdung, printed at Basle in 1511, the entire work occupying only fifty-six quarto pages, which contain fairly accurate pictures of the instruments then in vogue. Our investigations limit us, of course, to bowed instruments; and amongst these pictures we find the "great fiddle," and the "little fiddle," reproductions of which will be found in figures 9 and 10.

This "great fiddle," as will be seen, is of a somewhat grotesque shape. The middle "bouts" are very long and deeply cut, so that the upper and lower bends hang over to an excessive degree. The "f-holes" are represented by the two half-moon shaped holes cut in the upper part of the instrument, and there is a round "sound-hole" of altogether disproportionate size. The instrument has nine strings, and the way in which they are fastened, as well as the frets on the finger-board, remind us of the lute.

In the picture of the " great fiddle " of Virdung, whose drawings were almost exactly reproduced in the works of Agricola, Nachtigall, and S. Ganassi del Fontego, there are several conspicuous errors. Fétis says that this drawing (see Fig. 9) is in several points incorrect; the middle bouts are not right, because they are much too

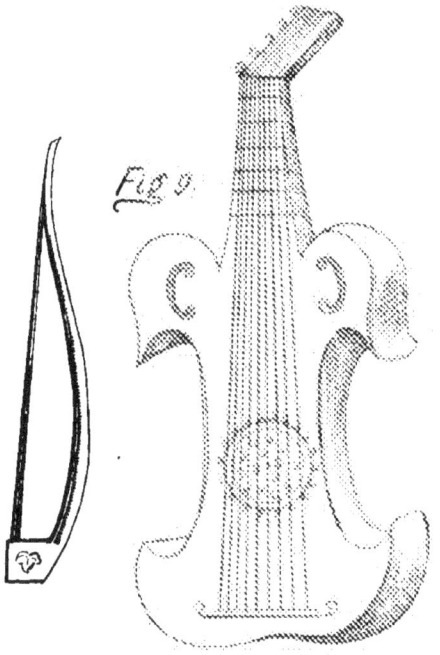

THE GREAT FIDDLE.

large; and the upper and lower bends are too small. A few violins and basses of the sixteenth century, still preserved in private cabinets on account of their rarity, show that the middle bouts are less than in the instrument as drawn by Virdung, although they were larger in proportion than those of the stringed instruments of our own day. Upon the question of the absence of a bridge,

Fétis further remarks that with an instrument built as shown by Virdung, the bow could not avoid touching all the strings at once; while the tone which it was capable of producing must have been very weak, as it is only by the angle made by the strings where they pass over the bridge that the necessary swing can be produced which carries the vibrations of the string through the bridge to the belly; and it is the bridge, itself vibrating with vigour, which imparts, with augmented force, those vibrations to the belly necessary to the intensity of the tone. Moreover, we must not forget that from the very first the efforts to produce tone from the strings by rubbing them with the bow have always employed the bridge as a necessary part of the apparatus. We find the bridge is a part of the original Ravanastron, of the Indian Omerti, of the Arabian Rebab and Kemangeh, and in short, of all the instruments which have been played by the bow. We are therefore driven to the conclusion that the omission of the bridge in the figures drawn by Agricola and Nachtigall can only be put down to forgetfulness or want of attention on the part of the draughtsmen who produced those figures. This is also the opinion of Fétis.

Although this explanation of the absence of the bridge seems the simplest and most natural, yet we cannot accept it altogether without question. The proofs that the draughtsmen were not over particular now and then are plainly enough to be seen; but if we accept the statement that the omission of the bridge is merely due to the neglect of the artist who made the drawings referred to by Fétis, this does not explain the fact that not only in the picture by Virdung (to whom Fétis does not refer), but also in both editions of Agricola's "Musica Instrumentalis," this "great fiddle" is shown without any bridge. A musical writer must have noticed, at the first glance, the absence of this essential part of the instrument; and would not a writer like Agricola have pounced upon this defect in his first edition, and had it made right when his book appeared the second time? Moreover, this same absence of the bridge characterises another instrument, the " key fiddle " (see Fig. 16), which is thus given not only by Agricola but by Prætorius as well. The " great fiddle" and the " key fiddle " are very similar in construction, and Prætorius gives the latter a place amongst those instruments which not only possess a bridge, but which demanded as great care in their construction as our modern instruments.

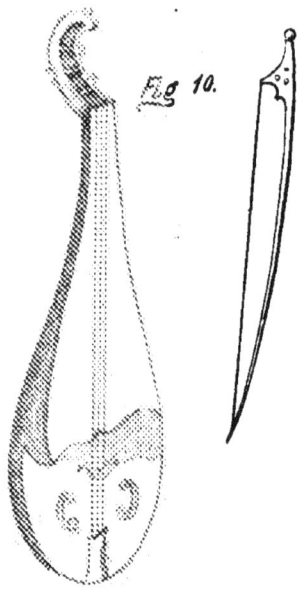

THE LITTLE FIDDLE.

Virdung's " little fiddle " (see Fig. 10) differs from our modern violin in the following points:—There is no fourth string; the great thickness of the neck; the mandoline-like sweep of the shape of the body; the altogether abnormal construction of the sound-table or belly; and the survival of the half-moon shaped sound-holes originated by the Mohammedans. On the other hand,

the "little fiddle" shows a decided advance in the scroll-like form of the peg-box, in the absence of frets from the finger-board, in the embryonic tail-piece, and in the bridge.
The use of frets was in the early days regarded as a practical and very useful invention, and it was long before people were willing to dispense with it. The fact that by the use of frets perfectly tempered intervals could be produced, does not seem to have had so much weight as the other fact that frets enabled an unskilful player to get some near approach to tunefulness. Virdung's "little fiddle" certainly made some progress by dispensing with frets; though the absence of these very frets, which we regard as a good feature, was by this old writer looked on as a defect.

Agricola's "Musica Instrumentalis," of which the first edition appeared in 1528, and the second, with scarcely any change, in 1542, shows no real advance on Virdung, and produces the same pictures. Agricola describes what he calls "three classes" of bowed instruments, which are, however, quite alike in the method of construction, and only differs as regards compass, number of strings, and tuning, as will be seen from the following list :—*

"THE GREAT FIDDLE.

Diskant: F, a, d, g, c'.
Ten. Alt: C, F, a, d, g.
Bassus: G, C, F, a, d, g.

"The other method with great or little fiddle, which only have four strings, which are thus tuned :—

Diskant: G, c, f, a.
Alt. Tenor: C, F, a, d.
Bass: G, C, F, a.

"Here follows the third way with the little fiddle, which has only three strings, tuned a fifth from each other:—

Diskant: G, d, a.
Alt. Tenor: C, G, d.
Bass: F, C, G."

---

* We give the list intact from Virdung.—*Translator*.

This last "way" corresponds to our own violin, if not as regards the number of strings, yet in the tuning, and further in the omission of the frets.

From the work of Agricola we learn that in his time it was the custom to divide the various kinds of members of the family of stringed instruments into classes, not only according to their size and compass, but that there was also a distinct class which corresponded to the compass and character of the various human voices. This custom had its origin in the ever growing elaboration of those pieces of music for several voices which had come into artistic use from the fourteenth century onwards. By the sixteenth century music had come to be most extensively employed in the services and ceremonies of the Church; and at the courts of princes it was usual to have at one time music sung by voices alone, and at other times to have the voices accompanied by instruments. With vocal pieces for few voices, each of these voices had assigned to it a particular instrument; but when a full chorus was used to produce the required quantity of tone, as was especially the case when two choirs were placed one at either end of the available space, then one chorus would have assigned to it instruments corresponding in compass to the voices, in order to make a distinction between the peculiar tone-colour of the two choirs. Instrumental music was therefore nothing but the echo, or counter-part, of the voices, notwithstanding the fact that nearly all the instruments which we now find put to so many and such varied uses were then available.

A work now very rare is the "Easy way to comprehend how to learn upon the Lute and Fiddle," written "by Hans Judenkünig, Lutist, and now in Vienna in Austria printed in the year 1523." Agricola only treats the fiddle family as of orchestral[*] importance, but

---

[*] The reader will not forget that the word "orchestral" here only means the playing of the same music as that sung by the voices as described in the preceding paragraph.—*Translator*.

Judenkünig, on the other hand, speaks of the fiddle as a solo instrument, and classes it as of equal rank and reputation with the lute. We shall see how important is this classification, if we remember that when Judenkünig wrote, the lute was held in similar esteem to that accorded to keyboard instruments in our own time. Indeed, Prætorius sets the lute above all other instruments; he calls it the "fundament und initium," and ranks it as not merely above such instruments as the theorbo, the cither, and the harp, but even higher than the "fiddles and viols." All through this sixteenth century the lute was in Germany the favourite instrument of kings, emperors, princes, and nobles, the highest ladies had it played in their presence; all songs of love and joy were accompained by it. One author calls it "*omnium instrumentorum princeps*"—"the chief of all instruments"; another names it "*nobillisimo stromento*,"—"the most noble instrument"; while a third describes it as "*regina instrumentorum*"—"the queen of instruments."

Judenkünig's "Instruction Book" for the "Lute and Fiddle" contains twenty-five pieces, suitable equally for the one or the other instrument, and is of the highest value to us, as throwing a clear light, in many ways, upon the degree of development to which players on the lute and fiddle had then attained. But Judenkünig has helped us further still, by giving us a picture of the "fiddle" as he knew it, and enabling us to see how it was handled. (See Fig. 12).

The instrument is somewhat large in build, and was tuned thus:—

The hook-shaped peg-box, bent backwards, enabled the fiddle to hang over the left shoulder, thus leaving free the

Fig 12

player's two arms. The " sound-holes " are like those of the later gamba, but are turned the other way about.

The instruments described by Silvestro Ganassi del Fontego (in his " Regola Rubertina, che insegna suonare de Viola d'arco tastada," Venice, 1543) is very much like the fiddle of Judenkünig, but very different from that found in Agricola. It was tuned thus:—

Discant: D, G, c, e, a, d^1.
Alt. or Tenor: $G, C, F, A, d, g,$
Bass: D, G, C, E, A, d.

There were seven frets on the finger-board, by means of which a chromatic scale of two and a half octaves could be played.

There is very little more that is noteworthy to be found in the known authors of the sixteenth century, beyond the fact that in a work by Giov. M. Lanfranco, kapellmeister at the cathedral of Brescia—" Scintille di Musica"—which was printed in 1533, the name " violino " appears for the first time. Another author was Ludovico Zacconi, who was a singer in the Austrian Royal Chapel, and afterwards in the cathedral at Munich; Zacconi wrote a book called " Prattica di Musica," published at Venice in 1592, wherein he stated that the compass of the violin was from G to b^1,* which proves that at that time what are now known as the second and third positions were altogether unknown and unthought of; and the b above the first ledger line over the stave was the highest note used on the violin long after the year when Zacconi's book was published.

The violin attains its perfected form in the " Syntagma Musicum " of Michael Prætorius, the second volume of which appeared in 1619.

---

* That is, from 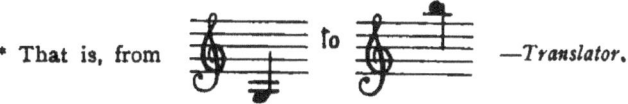 —*Translator.*

A few extracts from Prætorius on the family of bowed instruments cannot fail to interest the reader:—

"Viols, Fiddles, are of two kinds: 1, *Viole di gamba*, 2, *Viole de bracio* or *de brazzo*, and they have these names because the first is held between the legs, for *gamba* is an Italian word, and means the leg, the legs . . . ; and the other is called *de bracio*, which is held on the arm. And the *viol de gamba* has six strings, tuned in fourths, and in the middle in thirds, like the six-stringed lute."

"The *Viol Bastarda* is a sort of *Viol de gamba*, and is tuned like a tenor Viol de gamba, but the body is somewhat longer and larger."

Prætorius's *Tenor gamba* is shown in Fig. 13.

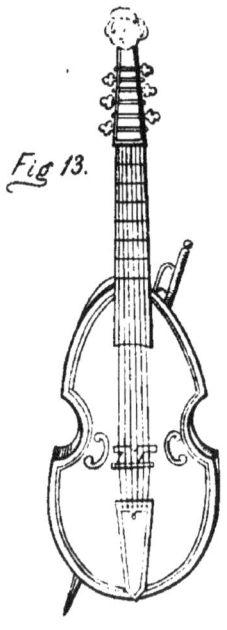

THE TENOR GAMBA.

Viol de Bracio, or *Violino da brazzo*, otherwise the *Geige*,* is called by the common folk a "fiddle," and thence *de bracio*, because it is held on the arm."

The scarcity of Prætorius's book is our only reason for placing these brief extracts before the reader. In addition to the above, Prætorius describes the "great lyre," the "little lyre," and the "trumscheit," all which tend to show that in the few years which intervened between Agricola and Prætorius the art of the lutemaker must have made tremendous strides to be able so richly to endow the family of bowed instruments.

But the violin of Prætorius's day could have possessed but little of the noble tone-character which soon after placed it in front of all other instruments. The reason of this is to be found not so much in the faults of the proportions of the instrument, or in the defects of its construction, as in the low pitch of the tuning of that day, the quality of the strings, and the unskilfulness of the players, who preferred to display their art on the lute.

So much in general on the state of the lutemaker's art, and relatively of music itself, in Germany at the beginning of the seventeenth century. The very fact that the actual name of the violin came from Italy, would appear at the first glance to imply that in that country the art of constructing bowed instruments had existed for a longer period and been brought to a higher state of development. This may or may not have been the case; but it is certain that, even in our own day, the people of our country † display a weakness for borrowing, without any necessity for doing so, foreign names and notions; and it is quite possible that, owing to the great number of Italian artists present at the courts of German princes, Italian names for German inventions and German productions were readily incorporated in the current speech and literature. *Proofs* that the violin had been further

---

* "Geige" is German for violin or fiddle.—*Translator*.

† That is, Germany.—*Translator*.

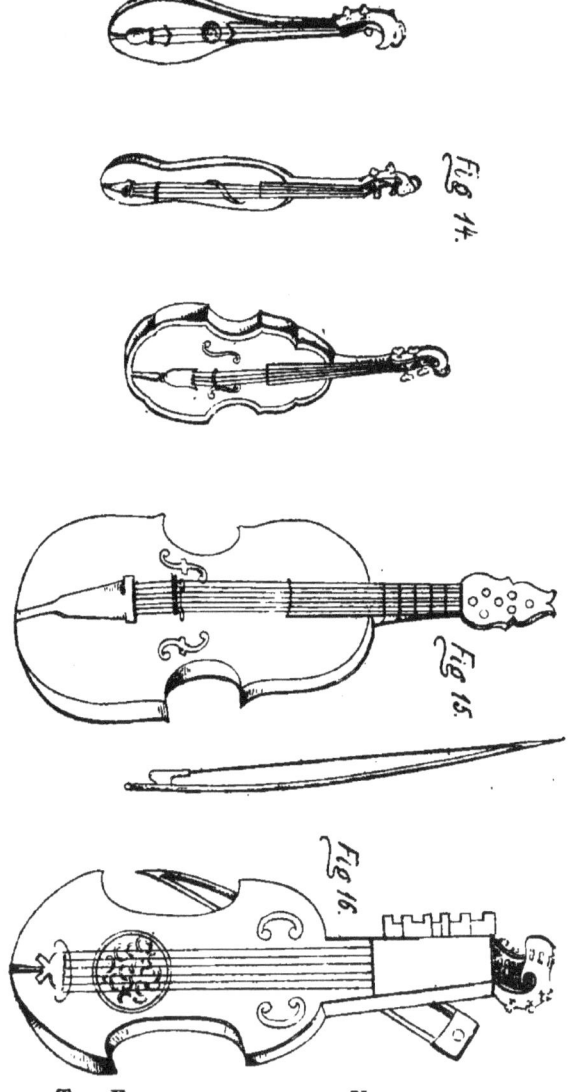

THE FORERUNNERS OF THE VIOLIN.

32   THE VIOLIN AND ITS STORY.

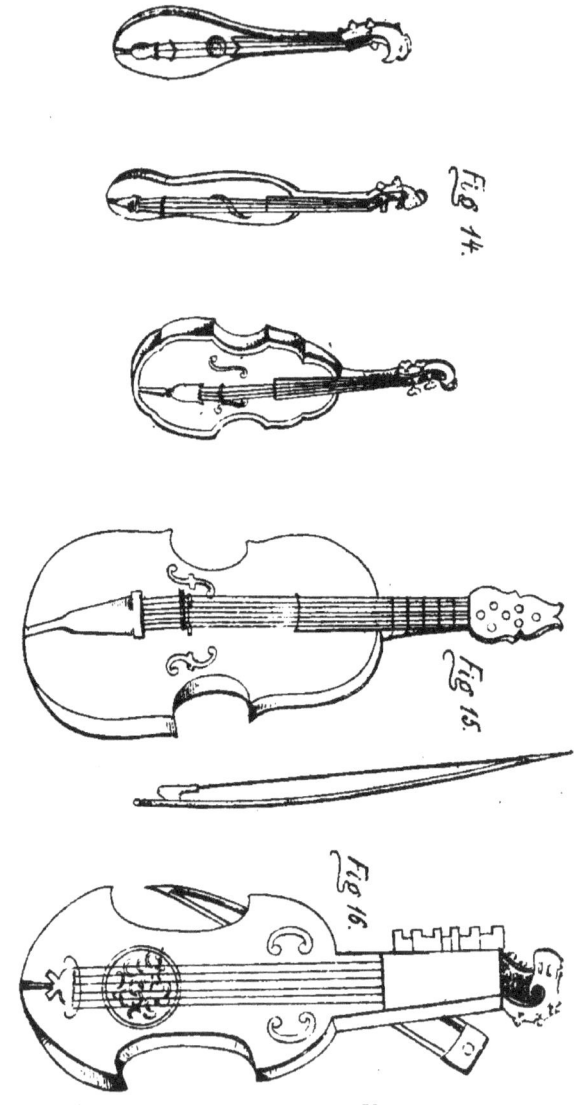

THE FORERUNNERS OF THE VIOLIN.

developed in Italy than in Germany are entirely wanting. When we read that Balthazarini, a Piedmontese, who died in 1570, had acquired such fame as a fiddler that Catherine de Medici sent for him to the French Court, we must not at once jump to the conclusion that he was a greater artist than Hans Judenkünig. Fétis went so far as to maintain that at the end of the sixteenth century the fiddle was but little known in Italy, seeing that its name appeared neither in the enumeration nor the analysis of musical instruments given by Cerrato in his book published in 1601. The first use of the real violin* is found in Monteverde's "Orfeo," which was produced at Mantua in 1607;† but the very use of the word "violin" by Monteverde leads us to believe that this metamorphosis of the violin into an orchestral instrument did not originate in Italy, for in his enumeration of their instruments which were to play the introductory symphony, he speaks of ten "violes da brazzo," three "knee-basses," two "contrabass viols," and two smaller fiddles "*after the French style.*"

When the immortal work of Prætorius appeared, Germany had already, long before, entered upon an epoch in her history more calamitous than any other; an epoch which destroyed the prosperity of her citizens, her time-honoured morals, and her political standing. Italy, on the other hand, had entered into possession of the noble inheritance handed down to her by Leo X. and the other great members of the Medici family. Here, under the happiest possible conditions, art was guided in the right direction to raise the æsthetic tastes of a talented people to the highest point of development. We shall show in our next section how these and other fortunate circumstances enabled a few genial spirits in Italy to elevate the art of violin-making to the pitch of its greatest perfection.

* Our author of course means *in Italy*, though he does not say so. He pleads valiantly for his native Germany, as befits a true patriot; but later on our readers will be better able to judge of the claim he puts up for his own country.—*Translator.*

† Mr. W. S. Rockstro says 1608. See Grove's Dictionary, Vol. II., page 358.—*Translator.*

34   THE VIOLIN AND ITS STORY.

PART II.

The oldest masters of the art of the lutemaker: Joan Kerlino, 1449; Pietro Dardelli, 1500; Kaspar Duiffoprugar, 1510; etc., etc. School of Brescia—the first violin makers,- Gaspar da Salo, J. P. Maggini, etc. School of Cremona—the Amati, Ant. Stradivario (Stradivarius) Giuseppe Guarnerio (Guarnerius). Pupils of these masters. The schools of Milan, Venice, etc. The German School: Jacobus Stainer, Albani, M. Klotz, etc. Founding of the art at Mittenwald. German Masters who followed the Italians, or copied Stainer. French Masters: Lupot, Gand, Vuillaume. The fortunes of the art of violin making, from Stainer to the present time. The experiments of the various masters; Savart's investigations. The decline of the violin maker's art, and its causes.

In the foregoing section we have stated that Prætorius was the first author who treats of the violin in its perfected form as we know it to-day. This fact leads us to assume that the class of instruments in question must have come into more or less extensive use in the beginning of the seventeenth century, but at the same time affords no help in discovering the period of its origin; and thus we are compelled to go back to the cradle of the art of the lute maker.

In this respect the fifteenth century furnishes us with one name only. According to Laborde, there was in

Brittany a maker of lutes named Kerlin, one of whose instruments, made in the year 1449, he had himself seen. In 1804, about twenty-five years after Laborde's work was published, this instrument was in the possession of Koliker, the violin maker, at Paris. It was more arched than the viols of a later date, the upper and lower bends were not rounded enough, and the corners of the middle bouts were blunt; instead of the usual tail-piece it had a strip of ivory, bored with four holes to hold the strings. The tone was soft, but dull. The label read—" Joan Kerlino, ann. 1449." Fétis thinks that the fact that in Brittany there were very many family names beginning with " Ker," led Laborde to believe that Kerlin worked in that province; whereas we are indebted to the labours of Vuillaume, the Parisian violin maker, for the knowledge that in 1450 there was in Brescia a lute maker named Johann Kerlino, and there is every reason for believing that this Kerlino was the founder of the school of Brescia, the oldest of all schools of violin making in Italy. The arbitrary conclusion of Laborde thus loses all weight, and the conjecture that Kerlin may have been of German origin must be left for some future writer to establish.

The oldest Italian lute-maker after Kerlino was Pietro Dardelli, of Mantua, who worked from the year 1500 onwards. A few of his beautiful viols are still preserved as treasures in the cabinets of connoisseurs.

But a far greater fame than that of either of these two, has fallen to the lot of the next artist, Kaspar Duiffoprugar, who was born in the Tyrol, and settled in Bologna in 1510. Some writers suppose that he afterwards went to live at Lyons, and that he died there. Various collectors in Paris still have beautiful instruments made by Duiffoprugar, including Bass, Tenor, and Discant viols, made by him for the Royal chapel. His works reveal an industry truly wonderful, and are of great beauty. Vuillaume, of Paris, had a 'cello made by this master, on the back of which was inlaid a plan of the Paris of that day.

Towards the middle of the sixteenth century we find Venturi Linarolli, who worked in Venice from about 1520; Peregrino Zanetta, of Brescia, and Morglato Morelli, of Mantua, about 1540; the latter probably a pupil of Dardelli. Some of his instruments, of about the year 1550, are still extant.

These old masters made only viols, of all sorts and all sizes, and their works in their original form have only come down in very rare instances, as they were for the most part broken up to repair instruments now in use. It was after the middle of the sixteenth century that the reduced form of the viol, the "violino," our violin of to-day, appeared; and about the same time the great Italian school of makers, which we now preceed to describe, began to take real form.

THE SCHOOL OF BRESCIA.

The leading representative of this school is GASPAR DA SALO, so called because he was born in the little town of Salo. He is the first artist whose *violins* we possess; and he was at the same time one of the greatest masters of his craft in the sixteenth century. The period of his greatest activity is held to have been from 1560 to 1610. He won great celebrity by his viols, 'cellos, and contra-basses,—a class of instruments which in his days were in far greater demand than the violin itself, although some very fine examples of his work as a violin maker are known. A truly splendid specimen of a Gaspar da Salo violin formed part of a famous collection of instruments at Milan, sold in 1807. Of another, which in 1788 was in the hands of the Baron von Bagge, Rudolf Kreutzer spoke with immense admiration and wonder.

The violins of Gaspar da Salo are of a somewhat large build, with strong curves, and varnished with a dark brown varnish; but their shape corresponds little with that adopted by the great Italian makers. The middle bouts are cut very shallow: the corners project but little, and are strongly rounded; while the sound-holes are large, and parallel to each other—a feature which is peculiar to the Brescian school. Gaspar selected for his bellies wood of an astonishing uniformity and regularity of grain. The most beautiful, and in this respect the most remarkable, specimen of his work is the violin possessed by Ole Bull.* This violin was previously owned by Rehatschek, of Vienna, who prized it very highly. Instead of the volute, or scroll, it had a wonderfully fine angel's head; the finger-board and tailpiece were of the old shape, now no longer in use. Ole Bull had it fitted up, and found that in spite of its great age its tone was like that of a new fiddle. Mr. Forster, an English amateur, had in his fine collection of instruments a violin labelled " Gaspar da Salo in Brescia 1613." The tone was clear, but not great. Fétis said that if this fiddle was really made by him whose name it bore, it must have been made in Gaspar's extreme old age, when he was almost past work.

Before Gaspar da Salo's time the definite form of the violin was not fixed; but it is obvious that it was through his productions that the present form of the instrument was determined. Consequently there are only a few minor differences between his instruments and ours—differences which only the trained eye of the expert can detect.

JOHANN PAUL MAGGINI, probably a pupil of Gaspar, worked at Brescia, his birthplace, from 1590 to 1640. He is celebrated chiefly for his violins. His pattern is large, the curves strongly marked: the belly is thick, but the back not quite so strong as the backs of Gaspar da Salo, with whose works his violins in most details are in agreement. The edges are but slightly raised; the varnish, notable for its fineness, is a clear golden brown; the purfling was generally double. For the most part his violins are famous for their grand, deep, melancholy tone; and they

---

* The reader must bear in mind that our author's first edition appeared as long ago as 1864, and the edition which we are translating, in 1873.—*Translator*.

have recently gained a certain popularity through one upon which Vieuxtemps played, although before that time Charles de Beriot brought forth great results from his Maggini, and at the same time fixed the attention of artists upon the maker.

We mention in this place a contemporary of the two makers just referred to, viz., Anton Marini, of Pesaro, who made violins from 1570 to 1620. His instruments were not made upon any fixed principles, and have but little value, being never sought after as rare objects.

There were yet two other artists in Brescia about 1580—Javietta Budiana and Matteo Bente, whose productions are not equal to those of Maggini, though a few of Bente's are occasionally to be found in the cabinets of collectors.

Santo Maggini, who must not be confounded with Johann Paul, though he perhaps came of the same family, worked in the seventeenth century. He was not so well known by his violins as by his contra-basses, which are in Italy regarded as the best of their class.

Other names of makers of this school are Tarisio, Antonio Maria Lousa, and Nella Raphael.

The Cremona School.

The founder of this school, and the head of the family so celebrated for the manufacture of stringed instruments, was—

Andreas Amati. His family was one of the most ancient and most highly respected in his native city, in the records of which the Amati are mentioned as far back as the year 1097. The precise date of the birth of this master is not known, as the register of births in the church in his district does not reach back to the sixteenth century; but he would appear to have been born about the beginning of that century. Thus, two instruments of Andreas Amati are known which bear the dates of 1546 and 1554 respectively. The first is a three-stringed Rebek, which is (or was) to be found in the priceless

collection of Count Cozio de Salabue, of Milan; while the
second is a Viola Bastarda, in the possession of the
already mentioned Baron Bagge. If we fix the birth of
Andreas Amati at some time during the first twenty
years of the sixteenth century, we shall probably not be
far wrong. A third instrument of this maker will come
under our notice a little farther on.

Who was the master of Andreas, or where his teacher
worked, is, like the date of his birth, also unknown. A
work entitled "Luthomonographie," the statements in
which must be accepted with all reserve, says that the
" Teacher of all the Amati " was one Giov. Marc. del
Bussetto (1540-1580) at Cremona, who, though probably
trained in the Brescian School, built his instruments on
quite different principles. Some maintain that Bussetto
was only a contemporary of Andreas Amati; while others
assert that before Andreas set up his workshop in
Cremona, he had worked as a pupil in Brescia.

The instruments of this master have a form all their
own, which is at striking variance with those of the old
school of Brescia. They are of small or medium-sized
pattern, with strong and well-marked arching in the
middle; very durable, clear brown varnish; and they
have fine belly-wood. We look in vain, in the fiddles of
Andreas Amati, for that power and intensity of tone
which so astonishes us in the works of the later masters.
This must not be regarded as in any sense a reproach to
his art, and it is impossible to overlook the fact that he
must have devoted much serious study to the task of
determining the proportions of his instruments and the
relations of the various parts to each other, so as to
regulate the quantity of tone in accordance with the
requirements and demands of his era. In Andreas
Amati's day, that power and fulness of tone which we
now look for was not required; on the contrary, an
instrument capable of producing the tone to which we are
accustomed would have shocked an ear accustomed to
the soft and gentle music of that epoch. All that was
required from an instrument maker was that he should

produce an instrument capable of yielding a weak, mild, but pleasing sound. And this virtue must be ascribed in the highest degree to the head of the Amati family; his violins and basses leave in this respect nothing to be desired.

Whatever might have been the number of instruments made by Andreas Amati, only a few of them have come down to us. Those which he made to the order of Charles IX. of France, were amongst the accessories of the Royal Chapel at the outbreak of the French Revolution in 1789; but after the famous 5th and 6th of October, 1790, at Versailles, all these instruments disappeared. Some years later a few of them were found by Cartier, and in his opinion the tone, though not powerful, was "full of charm," and the workmanship of a remarkably high quality.

The precise date of the death of Andreas is unknown, but it seems probable that he died about 1580, and from that year the instruments bearing the Amati name were made by his sons,

HIERONYMUS and ANTONIUS, and until the marriage of Hieronymus the brothers carried on business together under the name of "Hieronymus et Antonius Amati, Andreas filii."

ANTONIO (Antonius), who was born at Cremona in 1550, worked on his father's lines, though he, for the most part, selected for his violins the smaller pattern, and the larger but seldom. The violins made during the period in which the brothers were associated are highly valued and earnestly sought for, so long as they are in good condition. The violinist Libon possessed a violin bearing the label "Hieronymus et Antonius Amati, 1591," which on account of its charming tone was a wonderful instrument. The small violins of Antonio Amati have a soft, round, good tone, but it is unfortunate that a tone so pure and fine should be lacking in intensity. The first and second strings are the best of these instruments, the D string being somewhat dull, and the G too weak. The best and most widely celebrated instruments made by the two brothers are of a rare beauty of workmanship, and show the utmost care in the selection of the materials. The proportions of the relative strength of wood, the curves, etc., impart to them a fine, delicate, and pleasant tone, and the characteristic quality for which they are distinguished.

HIERONYMUS, in the instruments made by his own hand, did not adhere strictly to the pattern of Andreas; there are a few instruments of his built on somewhat larger lines than his father's, and which differ both from those of Andreas and Antonio. Though Hieronymus, in his own work, shows something of his brother's fine craft, yet he stands considerably below him. Hieronymus died in 1638.

Amongst the pupils of Antonius and Hieronymus Amati must be mentioned Gioacchino (or Giodfredo) Cappa, who was born at Cremona in 1590. He established himself in Piedmont in 1640, and founded there the school of Saluzzio or Saluces, where the reigning prince lived; and it is on this account that Cappa is known by the name of Cappa di Salluzio, or Cappa d'Assaluzzo. He made a great number of instruments, and originated an excellent school of makers, amongst whom were Acevo and Sapino, whose works were called Amatis, though they did not equal those of the Amati family. The best instruments made by Cappa are his 'cellos.

NICHOLAS AMATI, the son of Hieronymus, was the most famous maker of that name. According to the registers of the cathedral of Cremona, he was born on the 3rd of September, 1596, and died at the age of eighty-eight on the 12th of August, 1684. He varied but little from the form and proportions adopted by his family, but he was a greater adept in the art of perfecting his details. He differed from his father by adopting a somewhat smaller size, and also in his own peculiar arching. Between the hollow at the edges and the top of his arch in the middle there is a rise of nearly an inch; his corners are more extended outwards; his edges are beautifully rounded; his varnish, stronger and more flexible, presents a more beautiful appearance than that of his predecessors; the proportions of his thickness of wood to his height of arching are more accurate than those of Andreas, Antonio, and Hieronymus. It thus comes about that his tone possesses not merely the pleasing quality which characterises theirs, but is also much fuller and more powerful. A few of Nicholas's violins, upon which he seems to have bestowed more than his usual loving care, are truly masterpieces of the art. Those of his instruments once contained in the collection of Count Cozio de Salabue, at Milan, and which were acquired by him in the year 1686, are looked on as marvels because of their perfection of detail and the purity and fulness of their tone. Not less famous were the violins of this master in the possession of Count Castell Barco; while the Nicholas Amati used by the virtuoso Alard was one of the finest which ever came from that maker's hands.

Nicholas Amati left two sons, Hieronymus and John Baptist. The last named was born in 1657, became a priest, and died in 1706; the former was born on the 26th of February, 1649, and learnt his father's business. He adopted a larger form than the other Amati, but bestowed much less care on his workmanship, and stands in a lower rank than his father. He made but few violins, and one of his, bearing the date 1672, was his last work. Hieronymus the son of Nicholas was the last violin maker of his name.

The pupils trained by Nicholas Amati were:— Hieronymus, his son; Andreas Guarnerius; Paolo Grancino; and Antonio Stradivari. In addition to these there are numerous other makers who may be said to belong to the Amati School, and we shall deal with them in their proper places.

We have before remarked on the great results achieved by the two schools of Brescia and of the Amati. In the works produced by these two schools constant progress is manifest, although the highest point of excellence was not reached. The instruments of Gaspar da Salo possess a grand and noble power of sound, a majestic and penetrating but veiled and melancholy tone ; in those of Nicholas, the most famous of all the Amati, the tone is pure, clear, and lovely, but of little intensity. To combine the power, the vigour, the grace and charm, with the purity and brilliance of the entire vibrating body of tone, —this was a problem yet to be solved; and this was accomplished in the most wonderful manner by—

ANTONIO STRADIVARIO, who was far and away the greatest of all violin makers. He came of a very distinguished family, whose records exist in the annals of Cremona as far back as the year 1127. The actual date of his birth is not known, but the year in which he was born has, by what may almost be called an accident, been made known to us. Among the instruments in the collection of Count Cozio di Salabue, was a violin by Stradivarius,* in which the renowned maker has given his age as ninety-two, and the year in which he made the fiddle as 1736; so that we know at any rate that Stradivarius was born in 1644.

A pupil of Nicholas Amati, he made a few violins from the year 1667, when he was twenty-three years of age, in which the form of his master was accurately copied, and to which he affixed the labels of Nicholas. He first began to put his own name in his instruments in 1670, though he produced but little till 1690; and his biographer, Vuillaume, is of opinion that during this period of twenty years Stradivarius did more in the way of experimenting and studious contemplation than in making instruments with any idea of selling them. The instruments made in this stretch of twenty years varied but slightly from those of Nicholas Amati. The year 1690 marks the point of departure or transition era, in which the works of the great artist began to exhibit a style all his own. He then began to impart greater fulness to his model, to bring his arching and the proportions of all the parts to

---

* We shall continue from this point to spell the name in this way, which is the one most familiar to lovers of the violin.— *Translator.*

the greatest perfection, and to regulate the thickness of his wood with the nicest exactitude. His varnish gained more fire and brilliance—in a word, his instruments took on an altogether changed appearance. This was the time when he entirely freed himself from the traditions of the Amati School. It was in the year 1700, when Stradivarius was already fifty-six years of age, that he revealed the powers of a master in their most brilliant form, and the instruments which he turned out from that year until 1715 were, without exception, of an unapproachable perfection. He now left off making experiments, and, convinced that he had reached his goal, he brought to bear upon every smallest detail the most scrupulous care, and wrought every part with the most laborious and unvarying precision. For his bellies he used only the most carefully selected and perfectly grained wood, which he used in such a way as to bring the narrowest of the stripes, or " year-rings," to the middle of the belly. His arching is the smallest of all the Italian masters, being only half-an-inch high, on which account the table is made of just that precise thickness which will enable it to withstand the pressure of the strings, without, at the same time, suffering any loss of vibrating power. For his sides he mostly at this period used willow, no doubt because it is specifically lighter than any other kind of wood. His sound-holes, cut with a masterly hand, remain as perfect models for all his successors; and the instruments of this brilliant era of Stradivarius's career exhibit a perfection of form which is only equalled by the wonderful precision manifested in even the most minute detail. It was but occasionally, and even then only to satisfy the fad of some artist, that he made any departure from his fixed and settled pattern. Thus, for example, he made some instruments of a somewhat longer pattern than usual; in appearance they reveal but little charm, but the minute care in the workmanship, the assured calculation of the relation of the parts to each other, the brilliance of tone and grand power, are the same in these as in the other works of that period.

The instruments made by Stradivarus from 1725 to 1730, while still good, do not show the same careful and skilful hand as before. The somewhat higher arching interferes with their brilliance of tone, the varnish is brown; but the output also diminishes, for there remain but few samples of this epoch.

From 1730, or even from a somewhat earlier date, the characteristic stamp of the master entirely vanishes. The firmness and masterfulness of the hoary headed old artist had, as was natural, departed from him. Some of the violins of Stradivarius of this time show that they were simply made under his own direction—"*sub disciplina Stradivarii*"; in others we recognise the hand of Carlo Bergonzi, or of some of the old artist's sons. After the death of the famous craftsman many unfinished instruments were found in his workshops; these were completed by his sons, and have his name on the printed labels; hence the uncertainty and confusion regarding the productions of his final period.

Stradivarius only made a small number of violas, and these were all of large size. Their penetrating, noble, and sympathetic quality of tone is of the greatest splendour.

The violoncellos made by him are more numerous. They display the same ever-growing progress in workmanship, the same exemplary exactness, as is found in his violins. They are of two sizes—one very large, and the other of much smaller proportions. To the former class belongs the instrument used by the famous artist Servais, which is celebrated both for its magnificent construction and for its beauty and extraordinary volume of tone. Another Stradivarius 'cello, of the smaller model, was formerly in the possession of Duport, and is now* the property of the virtuoso Franchomme, who paid £800 for it. It is the finest known example of Strad's 'cellos, and permits of the execution of all the

---

* We venture again to remind the reader that Abele wrote forty years ago.—*Translator*.

difficulties found in the new style of playing.* The great size of Servais' hand made it possible for him to play upon a larger instrument.

The works of Stradivarius are distinguished from those of all other makers not only because of their superior qualities, but also by the extraordinary number of instruments which came from his hand. If with his violins we include the violas and 'cellos which he made, there are extant more than 1000 of his works. This vast number can only be explained by the great age to which he lived, and by the fact that he kept on working up to the last. Stradivarius, according to the Register of Deaths in the Church of St. Dominic at Cremona, was buried on the 19th of December, 1737, and he thus died on the 17th or 18th of the same month. He was of a tall but slender figure. His work-rooms were in the house No. 1239, St. Dominic's Place. By industry and economy he appears to have gained something more than a competence, for his fellow-townsmen were wont to say, "As rich as Stradivarius"; and, judging by the greater value of money in his time he must indeed have been possessed of wealth, seeing that he never sold a new fiddle for less than about £4.

Vuillaume, to whom we are deeply indebted for so much varied information concerning Stradivarius, endeavours in the course of his book to set up an entirely new idea, viz., that in order to bring the tone of a violin to perfection, it need not be played on for a long time after it is made; and this he endeavours to prove from a Stradivarius which for sixty years remained in the collection of Count Cozio de Salabue, was bought by Tarisio in 1824, and at length came into Vuillaume's possession. He says that this violin had never been played on; the wood of which it was made was of really

---

* Our author is here a trifle obscure; but he no doubt means to say that the small size of this 'cello enables a hand of moderate size to compass all sorts of difficulties. This is evident from his next sentence, where he says Servais had a very large hand, and could therefore use a large sized Strad 'cello.—*Translator.*

surpassing beauty, and the most extreme care had been
exercised in its selection. It was made in 1716; the
brilliance of the varnish was not dimmed; it was to all
intents and purposes a new violin, and looked as though
it had but just come from the master's hand; it was, in
brief, the only one of Stradivarius's fiddles which had
come down to Vuillaume's time under those precise
circumstances. This uninjured monument of the art of
the old master, which had been untouched by a bow for
the best part of a century-and-a-half, disposed in the most
complete manner, Vuillaume contended, of the notion
that the tone of a violin is only pure and free when the
instrument has been long played upon, for here, in this
new violin, were found united all the qualities most
earnestly desired—strength, fire, roundness, purity,
freedom of speech, nobility; in a word, this violin was
an example of extraordinary magnificence as well as of
absolutely perfect tone. On this question of the necessity
of playing upon a violin before its tone can be at its best,
Spohr, when at Milan in 1811, wrote in his diary that
amongst the fine collections of violins he found in that
city, he saw four by Stradivarius, two of which were of
the artist's best period. " The tone, says Spohr, " is full
and strong, but somewhat new and woody, and to reach
excellence they must be played on for at least ten years."

Stradivarius was married, and had three sons and a
daughter. The sons were named respectively Francesco,
Omobono, and Paolo; the daughter was named
Katharina. Paolo devoted himself to commerce, but the
other two sons followed their father's calling. From
1725 to 1740, or thereabouts, Francesco made a few
violins, which bear his name; but there are others made
by him and his brother which bear the label, " Sotto la
disciplina d'A. Stradivarius, Cremona." Omobono con-
cerned himself more with the fitting up than with the
making of the violins. He died in the early days of June,
1742. His brother Francesco only outlived him by eleven
months, and was buried on the 13th of May, 1743.

In the very front rank of the numerous pupils of

Stradivarius stand Joseph Guarnerius and Carlo Bergonzi. The Guarnerius family had already produced several distinguished luthists, the oldest being

ANDREAS GUARNERIUS, born in the first half of the seventeenth century. He was the first pupil of Nicholas Amati, and worked from 1650 to about the year 1695. His instruments are noted for good work, after the style of the Amati violins, from which they vary in only slight details. They are usually regarded as of the second rank of excellence. A 'cello by this master, which was formerly at Prague, is famous not only for the splendid quality of wood and varnish, but also for a remarkably fine and full tone.

JOSEPH GUARNERIUS, son of the above-named Andreas, worked from 1690 to 1730. Although a pupil of his father, he did not copy his pattern, his instruments more nearly resembling those of Stradivarius, whose contemporary he was. Later on he copied the style and pattern of his more famous cousin, the great Joseph Guarnerius. His instruments possess many good qualities, and are very highly thought of by connoisseurs.

PETER GUARNERIUS was also the son of Andreas, and therefore the brother of the above named Joseph. He made instruments from 1690 to 1725, and though his earlier instruments are dated from Cremona, he afterwards settled in Mantua, where he turned out many productions, which, however, by reason of being too high in the arch, and of somewhat careless workmanship, are not greatly sought after.

Another PETER GUARNERIUS was the son of Joseph and grandson of Andreas. Instruments of his, made at Cremona from 1725 to 1740, are still extant; his work resembled that of his father, who taught him the art, but they are poorly finished.

The greatest artist of this name was JOSEPH ANTONIUS GUARNERIUS, usually known as "Giuseppe del Gesu," because the labels of some of his violins bore the mark I H✝S. He was born at Cremona on the 8th of June,

1683, and his father, John Baptist, was the brother of Andreas Guarnerius, as is shown by his usual label, "Joseph Guarnerius, Andreæ nepos" ("Joseph Guarnerius, grandson of Andreas"). John Baptist Guarnerius would appear to have followed some other business, as no instruments bearing his name are known, while his great son acquired his art not from any member of the Guarnerius family, but under Stradivarius.

The famous Joseph Guarnerius worked at Cremona from 1725 to 1745. His first violins are distinguished by characteristic tokens of originality, though the form somewhat varies. It is a few years later that we first find violins of his which show great care in construction, as well as wonderfully fine wood, and a varnish which rivals that of Stradivarius. The instruments of this period are of small pattern, only slightly arched, and of splendid appearance, the internal details being of good fir or deal. These violins show a few blemishes; for example, there is too much wood left in the centre of the arching, which prevents the free and energetic vibration of the belly. Compared with the style prevalent when they were made, the Joseph Guarnerius violins of this period must have failed in strength of tone and carrying power. In spite of their variations in pattern, these fiddles reflect in their appearance the greatness of their maker, comformable to those which beyond all question belong to the third period of his artistic activity, although in their external aspect they manifest the genial variety and freedom of genius. To this epoch belong a few of Joseph's instruments of the larger pattern, which for their beauty of form, the most carefully chosen wood, the assured relation of the parts one to another, and the brilliance, elasticity, and fire of the varnish, are worthy to rank with the noblest productions of Stradivarius.

Immediately after this celebrated period of the artist's career, Guarnerius's instruments, almost suddenly, began to fail to show those characteristic features which had distinguished his prior productions, and we merely find in them that certain peculiar greatness which to the last pervaded his work. Such a change in the character of his violins would be altogether inexplicable if we had not heard (though by rumour only) of the misfortunes which dogged his steps in his latter days, and which were no doubt the chief cause of this great and lamentable falling off. The reports once current in Italy respecting the troubles with which Guarnerius had to struggle in his declining years, are uncertain and occasionally contradictory; but thus much we do know, that the end of this brilliant artist was not the end of a well-to-do man. Bergonzi (grandson of the Carlo previously mentioned), who died at eighty years of age, used to say that Guarnerius del Gesu lived a very irregular life; that he was slothful and negligent; that he was too much given to wine and pleasure; and that his married life was not happy. According to one report, which is unconfirmed, he spent a few years in prison, where he died in 1745. Other reports correspond with Bergonzi's story. It is told that the prisoner's daughter took him the necessary wood and a few tools, with which he produced some fiddles, which however do him little credit. This same daughter brought out the violins when finished, and sold them at a low price in order to provide him with a few comforts to relieve his distress; that she bought, first from one violin maker and then from another, the varnish with which he covered these prison-made instruments, and that these facts explain the varieties of workmanship and of colour which cannot fail to be observed in the instruments produced at this period.

The fame of Joseph Guarnerius in Italy began at his death; but it was much later before his renown extended to France and Germany. Vuillaume, to whom we are indebted for this information, remarks that when he was young the price of one of Joseph Guarnerius's best violins was not more than 1,200 francs (£48), whereas a fine Strad fetched about £85: but later on, when men had learned to appreciate the fine tone of a Guarnerius, and his works were more sought after, the price rose to 6,000 francs (£240).

Among the finest and most famous of the instruments of this master, the concert violin used by Paganini must be placed in the first rank. After Paganini's death on the 24th of May, 1840, it was found by his will that he had left his violin to the Museum of his native city, Genoa, where it was preserved with scrupulous care. After the lapse of many years Sivori was permitted to play upon it, in the presence of the fathers of the city. Very fine specimens of Joseph Guarnerius were also possessed by Alard, and by M. Leduc, of Paris.

Among the imitators of Guarnerius were Paolo Antonio Testore and K. F. Landolphi, as well as Lorenzo Storioni, of Cremona; but their productions are only reckoned as third-rate.

Among the violin makers of the Amati school who worked at Cremona the following must be mentioned:—
FRANCESCO RUGGIERI, who was the best artist of his name, and made instruments from 1670 to 1720. His violins show, in the shape of the sound-holes, one of the most widely divergent and independent departures from the traditions of the Amati.

In the direct school of Stradivarius must be classed his two sons, before referred to; LORENZO GUADAGNINI, 1695—1725, an excellent artist; CARLO BERGONZI, 1720 to 1750, one of the closest followers of his master, and who made some excellent instruments; and MICHAEL ANGELO BERGONZI, 1725 to 1750.

Further disciples of these celebrated schools will be treated of later on in their turn.

MILAN.

The oldest violin maker who worked at Milan is presumed to be TESTATOR the elder. He was a contemporary of Gaspar da Salo; and, according to the opinions held by some writers, he was the first who changed the viol to the violin. This opinion must however only be accepted with more than a grain of salt.

PAOLO GRANCINO, an able pupil of Nicholas Amati,

1665 to 1690; his sons, JOHN BAPTIST, 1690 to 1700, and JOHN, 1696 to 1720; as well as FRANCESCO GRANCINO, grandson of Paolo, 1710 to 1746, were all clever violin makers who worked at Milan on the principles of the Amati.

Of the Stradivarius school, the following masters worked in Milan:—CARLO GIUSEPPE TESTORE, 1690 to 1700; CARLO ANTONIO TESTORE, 1700 to 1730; PAOLO ANTONIO TESTORE, 1710 to 1745: and CARLO LANDOLFI, 1750 to 1760. Beside the above, may be mentioned ANTONIO MARIA LUCASSO; SANTINA SAUZZA; and FRANZ MILANI.

PIACENZA.

JOHN BAPTIST GUADAGNINI, 1755 to 1785, who in his early days worked at Cremona, was the pupil (and probably the son) of the above named Lorenzo Guadagnini: he occasionally worked here and there for the violin makers of Piacenza, and it is conjectured that in his later years he settled there.

MANTUA.

Beside the before mentioned Peter Guarnerius, Tomaso Baliestere, 1720 to 1750, Camilus de Camile (1715?), and Alessandro Zanti (1770?) were all of the Stradivarius school.

VENICE.

The decline of the art of violin-making in Italy begins with the Venetian makers. Although some of the Venetian masters made some good and well-built instruments, yet these seldom possess the valued qualities of the Cremona school. Of those who were distinguished amongst their contemporaries, the following may be mentioned:—

FRANCISCUS GOBETTUS, a pupil of Stradivarius, 1690 to 1720.

PETER VIMERCATI, (1640 to 1660?). He arched his

fiddles like those of the old Brescians, but he was not equal to imparting to them the tone of Gaspar da Salo and Maggini.

DOMENICO MONTAGNANA, the best of all the makers who laboured in Venice. He long worked in Cremona, then went to Mantua, and at last to Venice, where his best instruments were made. These were very broad, of good wood, and covered with golden varnish.

Of the Venetian makers of the second rank at the beginning of the eighteenth century were the following:—
SANTO SERAFINO, 1730 to 1745; SPIRITO SORZANA; PIETRO ANSELMO; the brothers CARL and JOHN TONONIS; ANSELMUS BELLOSIO, BODIO, the teacher of PETRUS VALENTINUS NOVELLO, who with MARCUS ANTONINO NOVELLO gained a merited reputation. The brothers FRANCESCO and MATTEO COFRILLER made concert violins of extraordinary power. We have still to mention DOMINICO BUSAU, GANTANO BONO, FRANCESCO GOBETTI (whose violins have very extensive tone), and ZANOLI.

TREVISO

has, so far as we know, only furnished one maker, PIETRO DELLA COSTA, an intelligent imitator of Stradivarius.

TURIN

has furnished CATENA; JOHN BAPTIST GUADAGNINI (1746), excellent imitator of Stradivarius; and DE GEORGI (1717).

LUCCA.

PAULUS PALMA.

FLORENCE.

JOHN BAPTIST DE GABBICELLIS here distinguished himself; BARTOLOMEO CHRISTOFORI, and LANDOLFI, also worked at Florence. Their instruments are well known by the thick coat of varnish with which they covered them.

LIVORNO.

ALEXANDER DULFENN, whose label was "Alexander Dulfenn fecit Livorno 1699," and ANTONIUS GARAGNANI, 1785.

BOLOGNA.

FLORENUS FLORENTUS; label "Johannes Florenus Quidantus fecit Bononiä anno 17," of the Amati school, 1685 to 1715, and MICHAEL ANGELO GARANI, an imitator of Stradivarius, and contemporary with Florenus.

ROME.

GASPAR ASSALONE was a Roman maker; the best of all the Roman violin makers was a German, DAVID DECHLER, 1690 to 1735. Dechler is classed by Vuillaume amongst the copyists of Stradivarius, while " Luthomonographie," on the other hand, states him to have been a pupil of Stainer, and relates that after working as an able artist at his native town of Salzburg, he quitted it and betook himself to Venice, but the climate of that city, and the jealousy of the makers already located there, made his life anything but a pleasant one. Coming forth one day from a church he was threatened with a dagger, and resolved to leave Venice for ever. He went at once to Rome, where he remained to the end of his days.

FERRARA.

ALEXANDER MEZZADIE, 1690 to 1720. Vuillaume says he was a copyist of Nicholas Amati, but his instruments appear to be imitations of Stradivarius.

DOMINICELLI, 1695 to 1715.

BRESCIA.

We give here a few worthy makers of the Amati school, whose productions, however, belong to a quite different category from that of Gaspar da Salo and Maggini:—JOHN BAPTIST RUGGERIUS, 1700 to 1725; GAËTANO PASTA, 1710 to ?; DOMENICO PASTA, 1710 to 1730, and TARISIO.

GENOA.

DAVID POZZURNUS, 1762; BERNARDUS CALCANIUS, 1748; PAOLO CASTELLO, 1750.

NAPLES.

ALEXANDER GAGLIANO, 1695 to 1725. Vuillaume says Gagliano was an undoubted pupil of Stradivarius. A story is told that Gagliano had to suddenly leave Naples, as he had tried to murder a man who had attempted to run away with his bride. When this affair had blown over, Gagliano returned to Naples, and set up a workshop there for the manufacture of violins, etc. A musical paper of his day described him as " a genius so great that it could not be measured." It is said that at his Naples workshop his two sons Januarius and Nicholas made such progress that by degrees they were able to produce instruments resembling those of Stradivarius and the Amati; but this notion wants digesting.

Other artists named Gagliano, in whose work we can recognise the Stradivarius pattern, were—NICHOLAS GAGLIANO, 1700 to 1740; FERDINAND, 1740 to 1750, and GENNARO, 1710 to 1750.

RAFAEL and ANTONIA GAGLIANO, who are descendants of this family still living* gave up violin making, and founded one of the best known gut-string factories.

As Neapolitan makers should be mentioned HANS MAN and DOMENICO SERESATI, though it is not quite certain where the latter worked.

VERONA.

BARTOLOMEO OBIZI.

THE GERMAN SCHOOL.

While the work of Italy was winning undying fame by the unexampled master-works of the Cremonese artists, a Tyrolian of the Nicholas Amati school, Jacob Stainer, was establishing an especial era of violin making in Germany.

---

* That is, in the "sixties."—*Translator*.

JACOB STAINER was born on the 14th of July, 1621, at Absam, a village not far from the Salmenstadt Hall in Innthale. The parson of the village interested himself in the poor but active lad, and sent him to Innsbruck to an organ builder with the idea of his learning the business. But Stainer was found to be too weak for this work, and on this account his master advised him to learn the lighter work of fiddle-making. By the recommendation and encouragement of this same parson, Stainer went to Nicholas Amati at Cremona. The fame of this master had doubtless already reached Innsbruck, as at the court of Archduke Leopold and Claudia de Medici a great many Italian musicians were retained. Amati was not long in recognising the talents of his pupil, inducted him into the secrets of his art, strongly pressed him to settle in Cremona, and to that end offered to give him his daughter to wife. Stainer, however, did not relish this part of the bargain, and run away to Venice, worked for a little while under Vimercati there, and at length settled in his native town, Absam. When scarcely twenty years old he sold violins in the Haller Market. He began, young enough, to unite art with love, and on October 7th, 1645, married Margaretha Holzhammer. His fame as a maker of violins continually increased; but as his wife brought him children almost as fast as he could make fiddles, poverty soon came in at the door, although we are not told that love had flown out at the window. Stainer determined to travel, and try to dispose of some of his violins. For some time he stayed at Kirchdorf in the house of a Jewish merchant named Salomon Huebmer, where he ran up a heavy bill for board and lodging, interest, and other charges, for which the Jew often sued him at law, and which gave Stainer a good deal of trouble for a considerable period.

Stainer's fame still continued to grow, and in 1669 King Leopold conferred upon him the title of Court violin maker, because, as the Diploma ran, " the repute of the trusty and beloved Stainer's good qualities and great experience as a violin maker had come to the ears of the King."

Whatever Stainer thought of this honour, it is certain that from that time forward he never prospered or kept his head above water. Huebmer, the Kirchdorf Jew, continued to sue for his debt, and at last he was thrown into goal, where he lay for six months. On his release the artist sank deeper and deeper into misery, until at last he lost his reason, and in this sad condition he died in 1683.

There was abundance of the finest pinewood in the neighbourhood of Stainer's birth-place; and he, like all the other great masters, used the greatest care in his selection. He knew, and studied for years, the trees suitable for his purpose, and would only have the oldest, which had not been cut down till their highest branches were already dead.

Although Stainer copied Nicholas Amati, he yet built his instruments on principles he had himself evolved. In particular he was distinguished by an unsurpassable elegance. His bodies were broader and somewhat shorter than those of the Italian masters, who as a whole favoured a longer, narrower, and more slender pattern. His arching was very high. The soundholes are shorter than those of the Amati, and finish with circular holes; and the corners, as was the case with Nicholas Amati, stand boldy out. The colour of his varnish is mostly red-gold, and his necks, instead of the usual scroll, often ended with a beautifully carved lion's head. While the tone of the Italian violins was clear, and at the same time full and penetrating, calling to mind the middle tones of the clarinet, Stainer's instruments, because of their pronounced arching, are somewhat weaker in tone, resembling more the flute, and therefore on this account not so fit for concert use as the Italians.

Instrument makers have greatly misused the famous name of Stainer, by putting his labels into their own mediocre productions. It is by these means that most of the pretended Stainer violins have came into the market.

The real and esteemed Stainers were divided into three periods by Lupot, the well-known violin maker of Paris, and by Cartier the violinist. To the first class belong the instruments made at Cremona, the labels of which bear the master's own handwriting. These are very scarce. They are known by their small pattern; the soundholes are small and narrow; the volutes are less than those of the Italian fiddles, but the points stand well apart; the wood is of somewhat coarse grain, and the varnish is like that of Nicholas Amati. A fine instrument of this period, dated 1644, was in the possession of the ballet-master Gardel, of Paris. Another was bought from Count Tranthuansdorf for no less than £415.

The violins of Stainer's second period, of which a magnificent specimen was the property of Alard, are not so scarce as those of the first period. Those of the third period were for the most part made by pupils under Stainer's immediate direction, and the labels are printed.

Vuillaume mentions one especially beautiful specimen of Stainer, on which he heard Sivori play, and which had an unusually splendid, sympathetic tone. Count Castel-Barco, of Milan, possessed a Stainer viola which was a grand sample of fine tone and excellent workmanship; and in the same collection were to be found quartets of instruments by Stradivarius, Joseph Guarnerius, Nicholas Amati, and one by Stainer.

It was stated that there was a MARKUS STAINER, who is said to have made some good violins. He is thought by some to have been the son, and by others the brother of Jacob Stainer. Vuillaume thought he was Jacob's brother, and that, although he was a monk, he used to help his brother with his instruments. Jacob had but one son, who died in infancy; but there is no trace to be found, in the baptismal register of Absam, of any Markus Stainer. Veracini, who next to Tartini was the finest player and the best informed fiddle connoisseur of his day, maintained that his two Markus Stainer violins, which he called "St. Peter" and "St. Paul," surpassed in tone the best Italian instruments. In 1746, when Veracini was travelling from London to his native Florence, he lost by shipwreck his two treasured violins and all his belongings.

Herr von Rennen, of Munich, had a viola of Markus Stainer; the varnish was dark, the belly-wood of beautiful grain, of large pattern, and of fine and uncommonly powerful tone. The label "Markus Stainer, Burger und Geigenmacher in Kuefstein, anno 1656," is in the maker's own handwriting.

To the school of Stainer belongs MATTHIAS ALBANI, who was born at Botzen in 1621. Gerber had one of this maker's violins, dated 1654, the label of which ran: —"Mathias Albanus fecit in Tyrol. Bolsani 1654." Fault is found with these instruments because of their high arching, and the inequality of their tone. The two lower strings have a nasal tone; the A is full and round; the E is strong and brilliant, but of a somewhat dry tone. Matthias Albani died at Botzen in 1673. His varnish was red-brown.

Albani's son, who was also named MATTHIAS, was born at Botzen in the middle of the seventeenth century. As he learned the art of violin making under his father's tuition, and worked in his shop at Cremona, he made many instruments which greatly resemble those of the Amati. Gerber had two of his violins, which bore the dates of 1702 and 1709 respectively.

Another ALBANI made violins at Palermo in the first half of the seventeeth century. No Christian name is found in his instruments, and no details of his life have come down to us. One good violin of his was found at Brussels, with the label, "Signor Albani in Palermo 1633."

"Luthomonographie" makes mention of a PAUL ALBANI, 1650, who always lived at Cremona; and of a Michael Albani, who established an instrument making business in Gratz.

According to Vuillaume, Stainer's best pupil was

MATTHÄUS KLOTZ, of Mittenwald. This, however, is not correct, for the art of violin making was established in Mittenwald by Egidius Klotz, the father of Matthäus, who came from Mittenwald, his native place, to Jacob Stainer, to learn the business, and then went back there. He was a clever pupil of Stainer, and his violins stand as high in esteem as those of his master. Klotz taught his son Matthäus all parts of the violin maker's art, but that vivacious and pushing youth did not at first take kindly to it. After he had laboured for twenty years in Mittenwald as an instrument maker, a longing to become perfect took hold of him, and led him to leave his home. He accordingly started on his travels, meeting with numerous adventures both gay and grave, and visited the cities of upper Italy which were most famous in connection with his craft, Florence and Cremona among the rest, returning home full of practical experience, and with the fixed resolve that Mittenwald must be a second Cremona. Some time in 1683 he began to put this resolve into action. He took in hand the sons of numerous leading citizens, instructed them in all the branches of violin making, and founded by these means a big manufacturing centre which not only enriched the town in his own day, but which is even to this day in a flourishing condition.

Matthäus was in this case a real friend in need. An insult which had long before been offered to the proud Venetian merchants by Duke Sigmund had caused them to cease to take their wares to the market at Botzen, and to carry them to Mittenwald instead, and, as the result, for nearly 200 years the latter city had enjoyed great prosperity. But in 1679 the market was once more transferred to Botzen; the thriving business streets of Mittenwald became almost deserted, and the prosperity of the place proportionately diminished. Then came Matthäus Klotz with his violin factory, which soon put the old town on its legs again.

The great abundance of pine trees contributed to the making of the fortunes of Mittenwald and the district.

Cattle-raising is scarcely profitable: the cultivation of the soil is hardly possible. The greater part of the dwellers in and around Mittenwald have become, on account of the start made by Klotz, engaged in fiddle making. The noble forests all around, as is the case with Ammergau further to the west, keep almost the entire population employed in some kind of wood carving. Klotz made the beginning; everybody knows what mainly supports the Mittenwald folk in the present day.

Besides Matthäus Klotz, there were several other Klotzes who are not unknown to fame; but the accounts of them are not so thoroughly in accord as might be wished. In Gerber's work, the account of the Klotz family is confined to this curt description:—"Klotz, a fiddle maker in the Tyrol;" Schilling, in his lexicon, gives no Klotz at all; Dr. Schebek omits from his list Joseph Klotz, the son and pupil of Matthäus, whose instruments are valued even in our own day, while on the other hand he includes Michael and Karl as sons of Egidius Klotz. Of GEORG KLOTZ, who worked in Mittenwald about 1754, and who turned out some very fine fiddles, it is not known whether he was the son or grandson of Matthäus. The most of the latter's works were made between 1670 and 1709. A Sebastian Klotz is also known.

It is said that the later members of the Klotz family were accustomed, whenever any violins came from the factory which were better than usual, and had the right form, to put Stainer labels in them, which accounts for the vast number of false Stainers in the market.

In Stainer's time there were several fiddle makers in the Bavarian town of Füssen; they worked, however, exclusively for Cremonese firms, and their activity only lasted as long as those firms lasted. It is to be here observed that the famous Viennese fiddle makers, BERNHARD and MARTIN STOSS, came from Füssen.

German violin makers have generally copied Stainer, though some have taken the Italians (but chiefly

Stradivarius) as their models. The following have imitated Stainer :—

STADELMANN, of Vienna, 1740. His instruments are most like Stainer's.

LEOPOLD WITHALM, of Nuremburg, 1720. He worked well and with great care. His belly-wood, very fine and well selected, is somewhat too thin, which detracts from the value of his work. Many of his fiddles are double purfled.

MATTHÄUS FRIEDRICH SCHEINLEIN, born in 1710, was a violinist at Langenfeld. It was late in life when he began, first to repair, and then to make violins, some of which were highly esteemed. His son John Michael, also an instrument maker, likewise lived at Langenfeld. His fiddles were neatly and industriously made, and brought him in his lifetime great fame, being of a full and pleasant tone. He copied Stainer's largest pattern, but lowered the high arching ; but his violins were poor in workmanship and were not lasting.

The following German makers copied Stradivarius :—

FRANZ LUPOT, of Stuttgart, a pupil of his model maker. He worked in his native city from 1725 to 1750, and was the father of the Lupot who eventually became a famous violin maker at Paris.

CARL LUDWIG BACHMANN, 1765, Court instrument maker at Berlin ; his productions are of good wood, excellent proportions, and durability of work, and were much sought after on account of their fine qualities.

JANG, 1774, of Dresden, and his pupil HUNGER, of Leipzig. The latter made chiefly violas, 'cellos, and double basses.

FRITSCHE, of Leipzig, is to be numbered amongst the best of the German masters, and was famous as a clever repairer.

FRANZ SCHONGER, of Erfurt, and HASSERT, of Eisenach, made good instruments, and the latter produced some very close imitations of Stradivarius.

FRANZ ANTON ERNST, a Bohemian, was in 1778 well known at Gotha, not merely as a distinguished violin player, but as a maker of fiddles in the Italian style.

French Makers.

The history of violin making shows that towards the end of the seventeenth century and at the beginning of the eighteenth, France produced only a few makers, whose works, however, were of but moderate worth—BOQUAY, PIERRET, DESPONT, VERON, GUERSAN, CASTAGUÉRY, ST. PAUL, SALOMON. Of greater importance than these is MÉDARD, who was trained in the workshops of Stradivarius, and then worked at Nancy from 1680 to 1720. He was the founder of the art of instrument making in Lorraine.

Another pupil of Stradivarius was JOHN VUILLAUME, of Mirecourt. He likewise made excellent violins, the period of his greatest activity being 1700 to 1740. Contemporary with him, and also a pupil of the Cremonese master, was AMBROSIUS DECOMBRE, who worked at Tournay, in Belgium, where he made some particularly good basses.

The foremost of all the French instrument makers, however, was NICHOLAS LUPOT, who was a son of the previously mentioned Franz Lupot; he was born at Stuttgart in 1758, and died in Paris 1824. His father was instrument maker to the Duke of Wurtemburg, and in his ninth year young Lupot travelled with his father to Orleans, where he was then established. In 1789 the younger Lupot went to Paris, where he was appointed instrument maker to the Conservatoire, and afterwards to the Royal Chapel. The instruments which he made for these institutions were delivered at the following prices:—Violins £12 each, 'cellos, £24 each. Some of his violins fetched even higher prices, ranging from fifty to ninety Louis d'or, and immediately after his death their price doubled. Like his father, he worked on the lines of Stradivarius, and in making his instruments he bestowed the most scrupulous care upon the very smallest detail. His last commission, of which, however, he did not live to see the complete execution, but which was taken over by his worthy pupil and successor, C. F. Gand, was to supply the Royal Chapel with an entirely new equipment of fourteen violins, four violas, six 'cellos and four double basses.

Spohr relates how he acquired his Lupot violin at Münster, while he was on his first journey to Italy. He was the guest of a manufacturer there, an ardent lover of music, who had formed an orchestra consisting of some of his officials and workmen. The leader of the orchestra played on a Lupot then thirty years old: and Spohr was so struck by the full and powerful tone of the instrument, that he persuaded the owner to exchange with him for an Italian violin which he had bought in Brunswick. Spohr afterwards bought a fine Strad from Madame Schlick, of Gotha.

In our own day, Gand and Vuillaume possessed undoubted talent; but the chief merit of their productions is that they are beautifully finished, though they cannot for a moment be compared with those of the old masters.

Vuillaume, who carried on his business on a great scale, and with all the advantages of capital at his back, and an active spirit of investigation to urge him on, studied deeply the theory which underlay the art of violin making; and he placed at the disposal of Savart, the French philosopher, the most costly and valuable specimens of the old Italian makers for the purposes of experiment, the full results of which have long since appeared in print. We have also Vuillaume to thank for practically the whole history of the art, to gather materials for which he several times travelled to Italy, and, with perseverance worthy of all praise, spent both money and labour in the task of getting together all sorts of information as to dates and other details respecting the great Cremonese masters. The results of his labours were given to the world in his famous work, "Antonio Stradivari; Paris. Vuillaume, violin maker, 1856," which was carefully edited by Fétis.

SPAIN.

We only know of one violin maker in Spain, CAROLE

Razenzo; and he by his name would seem to have been an Italian by birth. He worked at Barcelona towards the close of the seventeenth century.

England.

There is in England no special stringed instrument manufacture. Most of the instruments sold in England are brought over from Mittenwald, from Mirecourt, and from Markneukirchen; these are often very carefully finished in England, fitted with new necks, varnished, and then sold at an augmented price. There are however in England many good repairers, and not a few skilful connoisseurs, while London may be regarded as the best market in the world for old and valuable violins. The well-known firm of musical instrument salesmen, Messrs. Puttick and Simpson, often offer for auction in the course of a year from 2,000 to 3,000 instruments, amongst which are to be found some of the very best.

France.

A great development has taken place in the manufacture of stringed instruments in France. At Mirecourt alone there are thirty large factories, employing over 500 men. At the close of the seventeenth century, as the result of the labours of Médard, to whom allusion has already been made, the fame of the Mirecourt violin manufacture became widely known through his pupils, and at the present day it enjoys a wide-spread reputation. The Mirecourt makers do not confine themselves solely to the models left by Stradivarius, Guarnerius, Maggini, or the Amati, but make every possible description—German, and even English. Each of the Mirecourt factories has moreover its own speciality. The necessary pine, maple, and deal are brought from Switzerland, the ebony and foreign woods being imported from abroad. The Mirecourt productions are known for their great cheapness, their cleanness of finish, their elegance, and their fine varnish. The tone is pleasant, they respond easily to the touch, and the instruments are of peculiar value for conservatoires and orchestras; the prices range from 3fr. 50c. (about 3s.) to 150fr. (£6). Mirecourt is, so to speak, the cradle of the French violin manufacture, and the Vuillaume brothers, Mirmont, and many other Freuch makers were born at Mirecourt; it is, in fact, the analogue of Mittenwald in Bavaria.

As art products, the works of MIRMONT of Paris, take a high position. Mirmont gives promise of becoming a second Vuillaume, and seldom have we seen violins made with more care or greater acoustic knowledge. They are higher in price than those of the makers named in the last paragraph; his violins were £10 each, his violas £12, and his 'cellos £16; but in comparison with their high quality his instruments may be regarded as cheap. His tenors (violas), of an extra large size, had a full and splendid tone, and his 'cellos are peculiarly fitted for concert work. Mirmont, a man in the prime of life (he was first established in 1860) justifies the highest hope.

J. B. Vuillaume, of Paris, at an Industrial Exhibition held some years since,* exhibited two violins, copies of a Stradiuarius (Antonius Stradiuarius faciebat 1716) which caused the greatest astonishment. The greatest experts could scarcely distinguish between the original and the copies. The tone varied, but not in quantity, as is so often the case with copies. The tone of the original was clearer, weaker, and sweeter; Vuillaume's were stronger, not so sympathetic, but equally noble. The price of the original was £600; that of the copies was only about £16.

As a contrast to these exquisite pieces of workmanship it may be mentioned that, at this same exhibition, Schuster Brothers, of Markneukirchen, showed some instruments which caused universal astonishment by their exceedingly low prices. This firm exhibited violins at 9s. each, and some of fine (!) quality up to £3 10s.,

---

* That is, some years before Abele's book appeared.—*Translator*.

'cellos at £7 10s. and violins with inlaid work at as low a figure as 7s. 6d. each! Although made in a tasteless fashion, these instruments had still a good sound tone. With cheap instruments like these, the violin may well become a part of the children's school curriculum; quartets are no longer the monopoly of the rich; and the good influence of Haydn or Mozart can be brought into play in the meanest village home. Music makes people better, more moral; and the more of such instruments as these are made, the less likelihood is there of children growing up to be drunkards.*

The above sketch of the history of the art of violin making, and of some of the most famous masters of that art, sets forth only the leading features of the subject; but it is sufficiently extensive to show, amongst other things, that the art of violin-making reached its highest pitch of perfection in the hands of a few men of genius—such as the Amati, Stradivarius, Guarnerius, and Stainer. Further we find after a century and a half, that in spite of the universal progress made in the technical arts and trades, and the vast improvements effected in the manufacture of musical instruments generally, the violin is the one instrument which has not been bettered. In the manufacture of the violin the combined art and science of our own day can only show its highest perfection in imitating as closely as may be the perfect works turned out by those renowned masters. That the instruments made by the above named artists cannot be improved upon, has long been a universally accepted truth; and the countless attempts which have been made to beat the productions of these celebrated makers have one and all resulted in absolute failure.

In connection with these attempts at improvement mention must be made here of the experiments of Savart, the famous acoustician, of Paris. He converted violins

---

* Abele is quite right as to the power of music to brighten, sweeten, and generally improve the manners and morals of a people; and a volume might well be written on this topic.—*Translator.*

into a mere broad coffin—"two boards and four little boards"; the belly and back were perfectly flat, and two straight slits took the place of the soundholes. His idea was to have two vibrating flat boards, the vibrations to be communicated from belly to back by a little rod or sound-post. Savart thought very highly of his instrument, and so did many others after him. It need not be said that this "box" lacked all the brilliance of the Italian masterpieces, though it may have been suitable for the expression of the "softer sentiments." This rectangular chest, called a "fiddle," like many another box which enthusiasts have fitted with strings, had a very weak and peculiar tone of its own, but it was not in any sense the true "fiddle-tone."

Later on, Savart abandoned the use of this rectangular monstrosity, and sought by other experiments to unravel the secrets of the art of violin-making. He believed he could find useful data for his enquiries in the vibration numbers of the belly and back, as well as in the volume of air enclosed with the violin. By the liberality of Vuillaume, the Parisian violin maker, Savart was placed in a position to thoroughly examine a great number of the best specimens of Stradivarius and Guarnerius, not only as complete entities, but also as regards their separate components, and to make of them a most careful acoustic analysis. By means of a series of experiments, on similar lines to those made in physics to discover the nature of the vibrations of sounding bodies, Savart found that the note given by the belly and back respectively of each of the masters' instruments differed by a tone. In order to convince himself of the necessity for this difference of a tone, he had a violin built, of which both belly and back were of pine, and the tones of which, when set in vibration, were precisely alike. The quality of tone of this violin turned out to be thin and weak. Then he substituted a back of maple for the one of pine, the note of which was the same as that of the belly, just as was the case with the pine back. This, again, proved to be a bad fiddle, and the tone very poor indeed. If two

THE VIOLIN AND ITS STORY.   69

bellies, which when separate did not vibrate the same number of times, and consequently did not give the same note, were united they then gave one note. The same results came about with a right-angled closed chest.

By blowing through a small pipe into several Stradivarius violins, and thus setting the enclosed volume of air into vibration, Savart found that they always gave

the note 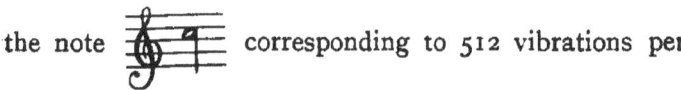 corresponding to 512 vibrations per

second, or the C flat of our own time. In the beginning of the eighteenth century, when Stradivarius made most of his best instruments, the pitch was half a tone lower than it is to-day, and thus—adopting Savart's mode of expression—all that master's violins were "tuned"* to the above note.

Savart announced his discovery as one of real importance to the science and industry of violin making. Unless these conditions were complied with, any violin would leave much to be desired. If the enclosed volume

of air gave  the lower registers of the instrument

would be bad; but if the note was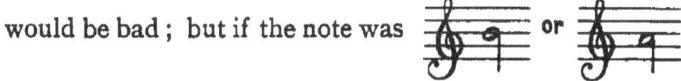

the upper registers would be bad, while the lower would resemble those of a viola.

In order to find out what effect the air volume had on the *strength* of tone, Savart had made a rectangular violin,

---

* This means that the enclosed air, made to sound by blowin through a small pipe, gave that note.—*Translator.*

with a back movable up and down like the piston of an air-pump. By moving the back to various positions he found which of those positions, and consequently what air-volume, gave the greatest strength and purity of tone.

The conclusions arrived at by Savart as the results of all these experiments may be thus stated:—

(1) The tone of the belly and back, in good violins, must vary by a whole or half tone, the note being between

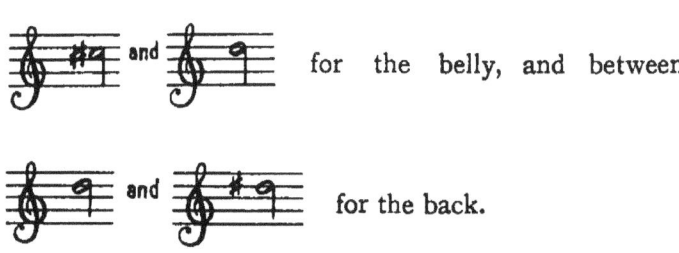

for the belly, and between for the back.

(2) The belly and back, which separately give different notes, must when joined together vibrate in unison.

(3) The enclosed air volume must vibrate in unison with the belly and back,* and as a complete system the separate parts of which stands in mutual relationship to each other.

(4) The strength of the tone depends on the air volume enclosed by the violin, which air volume must always stand in a fixed relationship to the other elements (the

note 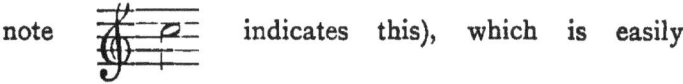 indicates this), which is easily

determined.

And yet, so far as concerns the art of violin-making, Savart's results were as good as nothing at all.

If the back and belly of a violin are of the same thickness, and equal care is bestowed upon them, they will

---

* This no doubt means "in unison with the belly and back *when joined together*" as in (2).—*Translator*.

always give notes one tone apart, because the maple of the back is denser and more rigid than the pine of the belly. Moreover, Savart's remark that the air volume enclosed in the violin must always give the note  would have manifested some ingenuity if the violin had only to produce this note C and its aliquot parts. But the violin should give D, D sharp, and all the semitones of the chromatic scale, with equal and equally good tone quality, and thus the notes given by the back and belly, separate or united, as well as by the enclosed air volume, are of no importance, but would seem to be rather a hindrance than a help. Further, in large violins, violas, and 'cellos, these conditions and proportion of the parts are not possible, and yet there are as good violas and 'cellos as there are violins. And yet further:—Zamminer has demonstrated that these very vibrational relationships of the bellies and backs of Stradivarius and Guarnerius, as well as the note of the enclosed air volume, are found in equal exactness in instruments which are not in any sense worthy to be classed with those masterpieces.

The nature and extent of the *arching*, and the manner in which the thicknesses of the wood are varied in various positions of that arching, exert a very real influence upon the tone of the instrument; and yet these details make not the slightest difference in the numerical and vibrational relationships above referred to.

Although Savart's new violin, which he caused to be played alongside a Stainer, may have had as good a tone as the latter, yet he confessed in his latest work that a violin without an arched belly and back had no penetrating power, and that the tone was entirely wanting in the peculiar and characteristic violin quality.

In the hope of throwing further light on the art of building the violin, makers have used numerous varieties of wood, as for example, cedar for the belly, and ebony and sandal wood for the backs and sides. A violin has even been made of tortoise-shell! All these experiments were of course much more costly than the ordinary violin, but as musical instruments they were of little value; and worse still were those "fiddles" made of silver, copper, or brass.

These attempts, together with the experiments made by Savart to discover the arrangement and purpose of the constituent parts of the violin, as well as the prior efforts of Chanot and others to give new features to the instrument, have, however, firmly established one fact, viz., that the violin model handed down to us from the classic Italian period is the best yet discovered, whether as regards convenience in playing or quality or power of tone. Savart has thus done a greater service, even though it be an indirect one, to the art of violin making than by all his precise rules, for he has helped to show that only in one way can that art be practised so as to give the best results. That one way consists in working as closely as possible on the lines laid down in the examples left by the great Cremonese makers.

Had the makers who succeeded these great artists been endowed with more stability and self-control, and been content to follow in the steps of their forerunners instead of seeking after originality and trying to improve on their pattern, the art of violin making would be in a better state than it now is. In that case a much less number of those noble instruments would have been so barbarously and unpardonably broken up and destroyed, and artists and *dilettante* who long for fine violins would not be put to such straits to find them. Nor would there have been the lapse of an entire century during which so very few really good instruments were produced for the enjoyment of contemporaries and the delight of posterity. In the meantime, the good instruments have been tried and proved, and perhaps a few later makers may achieve as great renown as some of the great Cremonese.

The decline in the art of violin making may be traced to two causes, which are in direct contrast one with the other.

One of these causes was that makers sought to improve upon the Cremonese, and went aside from the excellent rules of that school. Stainer, the prototype of the German makers, himself gave impetus to this desire for improvement. He made his bodies very high in the breast and back. A high arching not only suggests but positively demands less strength of wood. Stainer saw this well enough, and therefore made his bellies and backs weaker in wood than we find in the lower arching of Stradivarius. He fell, moreover, into an error of another kind, inasmuch as he allowed his high arching to fall away too suddenly towards the edges, and thus prevented the full and proportionate vibration of the whole surface. Hence we find that the tone of his instruments lacks the sweetness and roundness which the Italian violins possess, and more nearly resembles the sharp and "pointed" tone which is the characteristic of later German makes. Perhaps it was this very quality of tone which kept the Stainer violins so long in favour. This rapid fall from the arch when it got near the edges which, in Stainer's case was the direct and inevitable result of the extraordinary height of his arching, came to be regarded as an essential feature, and the depression round the edges became enlarged until it developed into a downright channel, from which the middle part of belly and back rose as a sudden roll or pad ; and the wood of the flatter part of the arching was made even thinner than was the case with Stainer's higher arching. These faults were very glaring in the productions of the older German and Bohemian makers. Even good makers like STADEL-MANN and GEISSENHOF (both of Vienna), and LEOPOLD WIDHALM, of Nuremburg, were to blame in these respects. The most pernicious fault was the thinness to which the bellies were reduced, the result of which was that after a short time the tone became thin, hollow and dull, and after no long interval the instruments were quite ruined.

All these clumsy and tinkering attempts at improvement have resulted in deterioration and degeneration. The Italian instruments rose in price when it was found they had no rivals to fear, and when so many good violins were ruined by bungling and blundering hands. What wonder, then, that men harked back to the classical, standard examples left by the great Italians? Even this resulted in people rushing to the opposite extreme; the Cremonese instruments were so much sought after, that makers sought their advantage in merely slavishly copying them. Instead of making really good instruments on the models of the great masters before them, as the Cremonese giants had to do in their own day, their unworthy successors merely attempted to imitate the outward form and appearance of those great works, and were content to impart the look of age and wear to inferior work. It was not enough for them to be imitators of the form and construction of the body of the violin, of the cutting and position of the sound-holes, of the turn of the scroll, of the colour of the varnish, and to produce the most illusory and deceptive resemblances to old violins; but they also attempted by scratching away the varnish, and the imitation of other defects, to produce the semblance of old age and constant use. The labels of the old Cremonese were also (and still are) exactly imitated and pasted in.

For about thirty years past[*], these "artists" have settled themselves in Paris, and have unfortunately found their way to Germany too.

There is one thing to be said even for this fashion of violin making, viz., that so long as only good, sound wood is used and the essential features of the Italian school are adhered to, no harm will result to the art itself; for in the end it can matter little to a player whether he plays on a new or on an old instrument, so long as that instrument is a good one. The skilful maker only hurts himself by these tricks of disguise and slavish imitation of the external details of the famous masterpieces. He cannot expect to make his own name, or to see his market grow more and more extensive, so long as he sends out

---

[*] Or, roughly speaking from 1830 to 1860.—*Translator*.

these imitations without his own label or some other token by which his works may be recognised. He must give up entirely all hope of fame, either contemporary or posthumous, and his descendants, or whoever carries on his business after his death, can inherit no good name to serve them as a recommendation in the eyes of the musical world.

This style of imitation or copying is beyond all question utterly reprehensible, if an attempt is made to impart to instruments right from the start those qualites of purity, sweetness, and ready response to the touch which characterise Italian violins already more than a century old, and which can only be the result of long, industrious, and careful use. Efforts are made to impart these qualities by cunning preparation of the wood, and by reducing the thickness of the bellies. At first the defects of the instrument do not reveal themselves to any great extent, and the object of the fabricator is accomplished when he has found a buyer for his bungled work. But the instrument fails altogether to last; it has no enduring qualities—no *staying power*, because the wood, on account of the artificial drying or baking to which it is subjected, or because of the thinness to which back and belly have been worked, cannot possibly retain that power of intense vibration which is so vitally necessary.

The soundness of this opinion is proved by the following indisputable facts.

(1) It is admitted on all hands that a violin made from wood which has been artificially prepared or "doctored," or in which the belly is worked too thin, not only cannot produce a really good tone, but that such tone as it does produce will rapidly fall away and vanish.

(2) It is established beyond all question that of two violins made from precisely similar wood, and in all other respects as much alike as possible, the one which has been for a long time played on will give a clearer and purer tone, and will respond more readily to the touch, than one which has just come fresh from the hands of the maker. It has been proved that it is not to the drying

of the wood alone that we owe excellence of tone, if the maker of the instrument has exercised judicious care in the selection of his wood. Much more does it follow that the fibres and all the molecules of the wood acquire through playing that mobility which is most suitable for vibration.

(3) There is no trace whatever discoverable that the wood of the old Italian fiddles, which the imitators most prize as samples, ever underwent any process of artificial drying or any other kind of preparation.

It is greatly to be desired that this degenerate method of making instruments should fall into desuetude. The experience and practical knowledge which time brings must sooner or later open the eyes of the musical world in respect to such bungled work, which—altogether apart from the arduous and most minute care vainly spent upon it—results in absolutely throwing away the really fine wood which is so often used in carrying out these deceitful practices.

After all said and done, there is no longer any doubt possible that fiddle makers must hark back to the good old ways of the Cremonese masters. It has long been thought, and is believed still, that their secret has been entirely lost. That "secret," however, reveals itself to every intelligent and experienced violin maker who will take the trouble to study with close attention the construction of those grand old masterpieces. If he will but choose good, sound, well-dried wood; if he will construct his violin with all due regard to the peculiarities of the wood he uses; if he will but make his instrument in its every part on the lines of a good pattern; if, moreover, he understands how to give to the bass-bar its exact proportions, and gives the requisite height, size, and quality—he cannot fail to produce a first-class fiddle. It will from the start yield a strong, powerful tone, and will manifest freedom of speech in all positions alike. With the careful use of years, all roughness will entirely disappear, and the tone will become as clear, as brilliant, and as free as that of his original model.

PART III.

THE THEORY OF VIOLIN MAKING.

The chief constituent parts of the violin.—1. THE STRINGS. *Vibration, Flexibility, Weight, Length, Elasticity. Harmonics. Tartini's combination-tones. Conditions of Pitch, Strength, and Quality of Tone. Gut-string manufacture in Italy and Germany. Practical Hints.* 2. THE TONE-PRODUCING BODY. *The conditions under which the tone is strengthened, not only by the vibrations of air, but by the vibrations of the wood itself. Molecular Vibration of Belly and Back. Practical Advice for selecting the best materials for Belly, Back, and Sides. The divisions of thickness of wood for Belly and Back. Anton Bagatella's Rules.* 3. BASS-BAR, SOUND-POST, AND BRIDGE. *The gradual perfection of Bass-bar and Bridge. The Neck, the Finger-board, the Nut, the Tailpiece, the Varnish. The Bow and its gradual development, up to the highest form by Tourte. Concluding remarks.*

In the previous pages it has been established that the excellence of a violin depends mainly upon the construction of the sounding body and its collective components; but on the other hand, every experienced player is familiar with the fact that the quality of the tone of a violin is very largely affected by the strings selected for it.

Belly, back, sides, bass-bar, sound-post, and strings, regarded separately, are of course very different things;

they differ in their purpose, and still more in their respective demands upon the art of the maker. It is now-a-days very easy to obtain good violin strings; and it is not difficult for the instrument maker to change a sound-post, alter a bass-bar, repair defects in the sides, or even to add a new back to a violin; but it is difficult, if not impossible, to replace the belly of a good fiddle so that the instrument shall suffer no loss by the operation.

But it would be a mistake to conclude, on this account, that any one of these parts was more important than the others, or that equal insight and care in working was not required by all of them; for it is certain that if any single one of these parts, whichever it be, is not perfectly suited to its purpose, it will affect the good quality of all the rest, if it does not destroy their excellence altogether. It may also be allowed that the finishing and perfecting of some one of these parts calls for more anxious care, more art, and more labour than the rest; but it yet remains true that the production of a good tone is conditioned by every one of the parts; and herein lies the astounding marvel of the organism of the violin.

The purpose of the following pages is to throw light on the detail work of the instrument maker, and to set forth the laws under which these details are put together so as to form a harmonious whole.

1. The Strings.

Vitruvius, in his work on architecture, well explains the spreading of sound in air as follows:—" Sound is a flying breath, which causes the air to tremble, and thus makes itself known to the ear. By these tremblings or waves the air is made to move in a multitude of concentric circles, just like the waves of water into which a stone has been thrown. These waves spread out from their central point in innumerable circles until they come to their limit of space or meet some obstructing object. In water these waves spread outwards in a horizontal direction only, while sound in air spreads itself above, below, and around in gradually widening circles.

Just as in water waves there is no motion of the whole body of water, but only an up-and-down motion of small portions on the surface, so it is with sound-waves, whether they are produced in air, in water, or in the ground. Just like a motion through a row of elastic balls,* so the sound-wave travels from one particle of air to another, each one passing on its motion to the next, and then returning to a state of rest as before.

The mode in which a violin string makes tremblings or waves in the air, and thus produces sound, will be made sensible to the eye by the following diagram :—

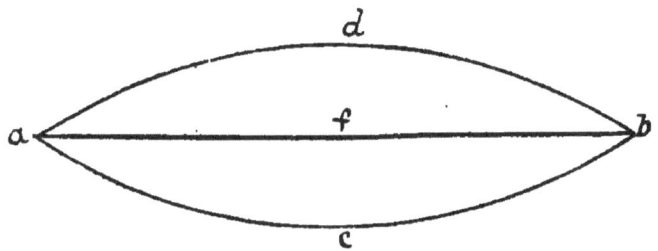

A string, a, f, b, elastic throughout its entire length, is

---

* It is a well authenticated fact that if a row of, say, a dozen billiard balls be placed on a billiard table, and another ball be gently rolled up to one end of the row, the ball at the other end will move away, without any perceptible motion of the intervening balls. Let the doubting reader try the experiment; seeing is believing. Ivory or bonzoline, hard as they are, are both elastic; and the motion of the ball rolled up at one end of the row is conveyed to the ball at the other end by the elasticity of the balls in the row. This little experiment is the best I know to convey to the mind an idea of the way in which one particle of air conveys its motion to the next, and thus causes sound (which is only the result of vibrations of air on the nerves of the ear) to travel, without any motion in the volume of air as a body. Indeed, the stiller is the air, the better does sound travel; for everybody knows how distinctly sounds can be heard on a quiet night when the air is absolutely at rest.—*Translator.*

drawn by some force to the positions a, c, b. As soon as the motive force is removed, the string, by virtue of its elasticity, seeks to resume its former position. The rapidity of its motion is greatest when it reaches the line a, f, b, and it cannot possibly come suddenly to rest at that point, but rebounds till it reaches the curve a, d, b, in which position its impulse in that direction stops. Its elasticity sets it once more in motion towards a, f, b, goes beyond it to a point on the side of the straight line, till its impulse is again exhausted; and so on, until the motive force imparted to the string at first is spent, when the string again rests at the straight line between a and b. This movement from the position a, c, b, to a, d, b, and back again, *once*, is called a swing, oscillation, or *vibration*, and the time which this one double movement takes is called the *vibration period* of the string.

If we say that the note has 256 vibrations, we mean that a string which gives this note, makes 256 to-and-fro vibrations in a second, the second being the time by which the *vibration number* of any note is fixed.

In a string used for the purpose of producing a sound, must be sought the conditions under which the *pitch* (height or depth), *strength*, and *quality* of the tone are determined.

The pitch of a string depends on its length, thickness, weight and elasticity. The longer, thicker and heavier a string is, and the less elasticity it has, the deeper will be the note produced by it; on the other hand, if the string is to produce a high note, the shorter, thinner, lighter and more elastic it must be. To put it briefly —the pitch of a string's tone depends on its dimensions and its elasticity.

All the more obvious facts about the vibrations of strings can be noticed by a careful observation of the stringed instruments in an orchestra. The viola, 'cello and double bass are all strung in a similar fashion to the violin,* but the strings become longer and heavier at each increase in the size of these instruments, because deeper tones are required to be produced.

If even deeper tones than those of the double bass were necessary, they could be produced by adding more weight. But this increase of weight in any string of a given length has its limits, because too much weight would entirely rob the string of its flexibility, which is one of its indispensable qualities. The covering of strings with silver wire, as with the G string of the violin, and the G and C strings of the viola and 'cello, gives the necessary weight to the strings without impairing their flexibility to a too great extent.

If the violin player wants to raise the pitch of one of his strings, he stretches it by turning the peg round which it is wound; and if the tone is already too high, he relaxes the stretch on the string by turning the peg the other way. But this method of altering the tone of a string is only available within very narrow limits. If, for instance, a violin, the four strings of which give these four notes: —

respectively, is fitted with four E strings, and the said four notes have to be produced by no other means than altering the stretch of the strings by turning the pegs, the stretch of the G string would have to be nearly twenty-five times less than that of the E string. An E string must not be stretched with greater force than is equal to a weight of 25lbs. hung on the string; a weight of 29lbs. would break it. The amount of stretch for the G string on this basis would be 1lb. only; and,

---

* This of course refers to the four-stringed double bass used in Germany, and not to the English three-stringed instrument.— *Translator.*

altogether apart from the fact that such unequal pressure on the belly would quite ruin any instrument, the tone of the G string under such circumstances would hardly be a musical tone at all.

No evidence as to the effect of the length of a string upon its pitch is more easily obtainable than to watch a violin player; his left hand is in constant motion, passing along the strings on the finger-board and back again, according to whether he wants to play a high or low note.

Every alteration in the weight, the elasticity, or the length of a string, has a corresponding effect upon its pitch. Mersenne, in the seventeenth century, first determined the relation of each of these three elements to the movements of a string, and their respective effects in fixing its vibration number. Pythagoras knew, ages before Mersenne's time, that by lightly stopping a string at half its length it gave the octave of its open sound, and that by stopping it at one third of its length it gave a note an octave and a fifth above its open sound; but the French philosopher found that the vibration number of the string was doubled when it was stopped in the middle, and trebled when it was stopped at one third of its length. In other words, the vibration number of a string increases in proportion as its length is diminished.

This brings us to the fact that stringed instruments, in addition to the tones obtained by the free vibration of their strings by bowing and stopping, possess a still higher register of tones called Harmonics. The player who desires to play the E a double octave above the tone of his open E string, stops that string lightly with his finger (without pressing the string on the finger board) at one quarter of its length, and gives the string a light but firm stroke with his bow, at one-eighth of the length of the string from the bridge. By similar light fingering in other positions, various harmonics may be produced, as shown in the following table:—

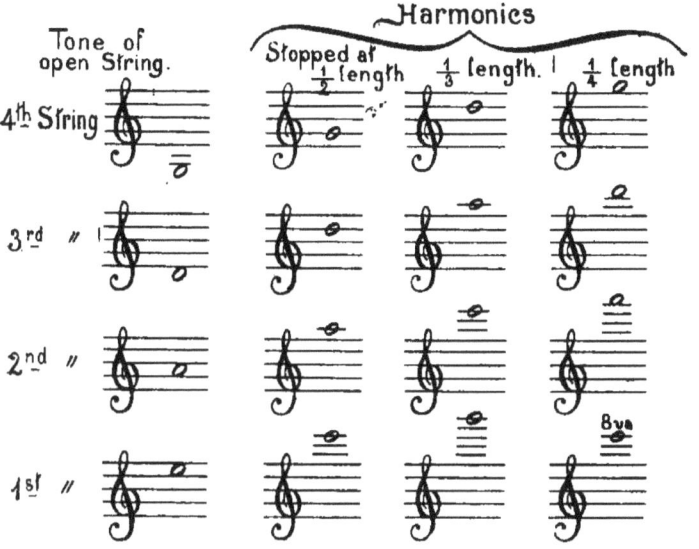

Other harmonic notes may be produced by stopping the string firmly with the first finger, and lightly stopping off with the fourth finger one fourth of the length of the sounding portion of the string, which gives the double octave of the note stopped with the first finger.

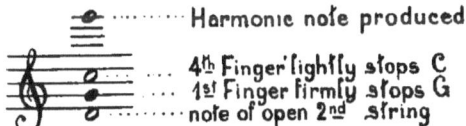

At this point we will refer to the so-called "combination tones." Although these were mentioned by German authors long before the time of Tartini, their discovery is usually ascribed to him, and they are therefore called "Tartini tones."

Every violin player must have observed that when he is playing strong and pure double-stops, these are accompanied by a third tone which is distinctly audible; this tone is not part of his purpose, and, indeed, it does not lie within the compass of his instrument. A similar phenomenon may be produced by two properly tuned metal rods, two flutes, two organ pipes, and so on, and it is known that the Abbé Vogler put this phenomenon into practical use in connection with the organ.

The origin of these combination tones may be thus explained:—When the difference between the vibration numbers of two notes is large enough to permit of their standing in a simple harmonic ratio to each other, there periodically comes a time when two vibrations, one belonging to each note, occur together. When this happens, the player will no longer hear merely the two notes which he is playing, but a third and deeper note made by the vibrations which occur each time the vibrations of the two notes played fall together, or happen at precisely the same period.

Take two notes, the vibration numbers of which are respectively 400 and 500 per second (a major third in this case). Then, when the lower note has made four vibrations, the upper note will have made five; and the fourth of the one and the fifth of the other will happen together, and mutually strengthen or augment each other. This strengthening process occurs precisely 100 times per second, and 100 is the vibration number of the combination tone thus produced, which will be a double octave below the lower of the two notes. The two notes are two separate wave systems, and the combination tone is a third wave system resulting from the fourth wave of the lower note coinciding with the fifth wave of the higher note 100 times in every second. The following little diagram will serve to make this clear:—

```
          *            *            *
1)    .  .  .  .  .  .  .  .  .  .
2)    .  .  .  .  .  .  .  .  .  .  .
3)    .            .            .
```

The points in the upper row show the waves of the

lower note; those in the second row the waves of the higher note; and those in the third row the waves of the combination tone, which are formed whenever the waves of the first and second rows coincide, as at the places marked *. According to the same law, combination tones are engendered by certain other intervals.

The *strength* of a tone depends on the *width* of the swing or vibration. The greater is the force which causes the string to vibrate, and takes it out of its position a, f, b (see former diagram, page 79), the greater of course will be the width of the swing or vibration and the louder the string will sound. Every increase or decrease in this width of swing will cause a corresponding increase or decrease in the *volume* of tone, without in the smallest degree altering the *number* of vibrations; in other words, the *quantity* of tone may change without any change of *pitch*.

The greater is the innate elasticity of a string, the more readily is it capable of a wide swing. The gut strings used for the violin family are peculiarly adapted, by reason of their great elasticity, to the purpose for which they are used. While a metal thread, or wire, will break before it can be stretched one-half per cent. of its length, a good gut string will stretch from five to twelve per cent. of its length, and return to its original length as soon as the stretching force ceases to act.

A violin may be fitted with strings which are either too weak or too strong for it, and in either case there is corresponding disadvantage. Strings too weak will require too little stretching, and strings too strong will want too much. The former offer too little resistance to the stroke of the bow; the latter offer too much. The practised player can at once judge, by the mere pressure of his finger on the string so as to make it touch the fingerboard, and without touching the string with the bow, whether it possesses just that amount of elasticity —no more and no less—which his instrument needs in order to bring out every possible shade and gradation of tone.

Just as the number of vibrations of a string per second fixes the pitch of the tone, and the width of those vibrations fixes its loudness or softness, so is the *quality* of the tone fixed by the *form* which the vibration takes. The more regular and even the form of the vibrations, the purer and finer is the quality of tone; the more irregular is the form of the vibrations, the more does that irregularity reveal itself in the tone-colour, or tone-quality, of the sound produced. It is the *form* of the vibrations alone which makes the difference between the soft, sibilant tone of the flute, the "biting" tone of the violin, and the piercing tone of the trumpet.

The strength and quality of tone of the strings of the violin are not, however, the only conditions necessary to produce the true violin tone; the "*resonance-body*," or body of the violin itself, is by far the most important factor. But even though the body of the violin may unite in itself, from the constructive and other points of view, every good quality that can be desired, the faulty stringing of the instrument will prevent those good qualities from showing themselves to the greatest advantage. Above all things, in addition to suitable strength and power to sustain stretching, a string must possess perfect equality if it is to yield a pure and fine tone. It may, therefore, be of interest to look closely at the very careful mode of operation which is necessary for the production of good violin strings.

In this manufacture the Italians stand easily first. Of the strings of the violin, the first, or E string, is the one which needs the greatest care in manufacture and finish, and the best—indeed, the only first strings suitable for solo playing—come from Italy. All attempts in more northern countries to produce E strings of the goodness, delicacy, and equality of the Italian firsts, have been up to now, and are likely to remain, absolute failures, for they lack the one vital and indispensable material—the peculiar quality of gut.

It is a theory well grounded on experience, that the membranes of thin animals are more ductile and more tenacious—tougher, in short—than those of fat ones. The thinness of the animal must not, however, be the result of under-feeding or defective nourishment, for in that case its membranes will be as unsuitable as, or even more unsuitable than, those obtained from fat or overfed animals.

The Neapolitans use for first strings only the gut of lambs, from seven to eight months old; and in no case must the lambs be over a year old. In Germany, the gut of lambs of that age cannot possibly be obtained in any quantity, as they are very seldom killed so young. In France and Germany alike the gut of sheep and calves is used, and both are too thick to make good E strings.

Angelo Angelucci, the founder of the Neapolitan string industry, is said to have employed in Naples alone over one hundred men whose sole duty it was to visit daily the slaughter-houses where the lambs and goats were killed, and buy the entrails of each animal. These entrails were at once cleansed and purified, lest the gut should turn a dark colour.

The entrails are sorted out into nine classes of varying quality and strength, the finest and slenderest pieces being selected for the best strings. The gut is sometimes fifty feet long, and the strong, thick ends are always cut off.

The great point is next to free the gut from all foreign constituents, from the mucous membrane, and from all appendages whatever. This can only be accomplished by a kind of induced putrefaction or maceration, for which a high and uniform temperature is necessary. In Italy the period from Easter to October is the best for string manufacture. The production of strings from gut is the result of a kind of fermentation, and therefore, as we have just observed, a uniformly high temperature is an absolute necessity; and even in Italy sudden changes of temperature will cause the operation to fail.

The selected pieces of gut of one quality are then put for twenty-four hours into fresh water, which must frequently be changed.

The pieces of macerated or fermented entrails are then drawn over a board, under the pressure of the rounded edge of a kind of knife, which takes off all the outer skin in long strips, clears away all mucus, and turns the gut into a transparent membrane. All these operations up to now have, however, only been preliminaries to the special preparation of the material for strings.

This special preparation consists of a corrosive mixture, called "aqua fortis" in the Italian manufacture. This mixture varies, and is bound to vary, in different countries. In Italy the lees of wine, diluted with water, are used.

The preparation of the gut in this corrosive mixture goes on during eight days, the weakest "lye" being used at first, and the strength increased up to the strongest. The secret of the Italian string manufacture lies precisely in the use of this "lye," and in the different strengths to be applied as the process goes on. According to one author, De la Lande, the weakest mixture consists of four parts of lees to two hundred parts of water, and the strongest of twenty parts of lees to two hundred parts of water.

Ten pieces only of the gut are laid in the weakest mixture, which has to be renewed four times daily, while the pieces are taken out of the vessel, briskly shaken about, and hung up for an hour in the open air. As above stated, the strength of the mixture is augmented daily, until the highest strength is reached on the eighth day. While these operations are going on, the pieces of gut gradually become clearer and purer, rise more and more in the liquid, until at last they float in water. This is the point at which the pieces must be stretched without delay, after which they are soaked in fresh water to free them from all traces of the "lye."

English, French, and German string makers, instead of wine lees, use a mixture of potash and water, which is clarified with alum when necessary. As often as this lye is changed, the gut is continuously drawn between the finger and a tailor's thimble, and so cleansed. The effect of the lye is quicker in this case, but it is quite another question whether the results are equal to those produced in Italy.

The gut strips are then wound upon a common ropemaker's wheel, of about three feet diameter; and it is essential, during this winding, that the operator shall constantly pass the strips between his two fingers, so as to discover any uneven places, and to assure himself that the piece is perfectly cylindrical.

For the higher mandoline strings two strips of gut are used; for the violin E string, three or four pieces; four for the A string, and six to nine for the D string. The thinner the string is to be, the more tightly must the strips be wound round the wheel. Two, three, and in some cases four, windings are necessary.

After the strips have been drawn out tightly by the wheel, and in order to secure the effects of the winding while the strips are still moist, they are stretched on a wooden frame five feet long and two feet wide. This frame is fitted with little wooden pegs, and on one of these pegs a strip is fastened, and then drawn out as far as it will reach and secured to another peg.

While thus tightly stretched, the strings (as they may now be described) are taken into what is called the "sulphur room," a chamber about twelve feet square, which is so heated that the strings will be nearly, though not quite, dry in twenty-four hours. When they are about half dry, which is usually in somewhere about fourteen hours, about two and a half pounds of sulphur, in a bowl, is set burning, and burns for six hours. At the end of the twenty-four hours the now whitened strings are removed from the sulphur chamber, and again put upon the wheel for a further and final stretching, and are then burnished. For the thicker strings, the sulphuring, winding, and burnishing processes have to be once or twice repeated, and the strings allowed to dry in the open air, which in fine warm weather takes five or six hours.

The finished strings are then anointed with fine olive

oil, cut into pieces from six to eight feet long, and rolled on a wooden cylinder in the form in which they are sent to market.

It is open to doubt whether this oiling process is worth the trouble it takes; and it is certain that a string does not yield its proper tone till all the oil is removed. The sulphur drying is also of questionable value; true it makes the strings clear and white, but in the course of time the string is damaged by it. Priali, of Padua, does not use sulphur at all, and yet his strings, when strung up for playing, are found to be clear and pure.

A good violin string must be of a perfectly cylindrical and homogenous form, without swellings or knots. It must be transparent, must not lose its colour or transparency when tuned up to pitch; and must, when screwed up and stretched nearly to the breaking point, return to its normal length when set free from pressure. A good string, stretched to its breaking point, will break suddenly and without any warning, just as is the case with steel wire.

The manufacture of strings, first established by the Italians, has on several occasions received the notice of governments. In the year 1822 a prize of 1,500 francs was offered in Paris to him who should perfect the art of preparing the entrails of animals, not only with a view to their serving as food, but also as regards their use as strings for musical instruments. But the problem was only half solved,* and when a later prize of 2,000 francs was offered, it was not won. The fact is, that England, France, and Germany cannot make E violin strings equal to the best Italian strings. We say *the best*; for even of the dearest and most carefully made Italian "firsts" it may be said that only about half of them deserve this description. Baillot has placed it on record that of a bundle of firsts made by Guida, of Naples, only half were fit for concert use.

---

* Presumably the food half was solved, but the string half not solved; Abele does not say this, but clearly implies it.—*Translator.*

The best violin firsts are made by Priali, of Padua; and there are most excellent strings made in the factories of Naples, Rome, and Milan.

So far as regards string manufacture in Germany, it is quite certain that with the requisite care we can produce A, D, and G strings equal to those of the Italian factories. But we must get our E strings from Italy—those at any rate, which are used by virtuosi for concert-playing, so long as we neglect to use the entrails of young and thin lambs, and fail to bestow as much attention to temperature during the process of fermentation as the Italians do.

The remarks of Spohr, in his well-known "Autobiography," on the subject of the selection of strings, are worthy the close attention of all violin players. For the accurate adjustment of the proportionate thickness of the four strings, a string-gauge is always necessary.*

As gut strings, if kept too long, lose their colour and elasticity (and the thinnest strings lose them soonest), it is never advisable to lay in a stock which will last longer than five or six months. Old and "exhausted" strings may be known by their yellow, faded look, and by their want of elasticity.

Strings should be (1) pure in themselves, and (2) pure in fifths.

A string is pure in itself (without overtones), as we have already stated, when its vibrations are regular and normal; and the vibrations are only regular and normal when the string is throughout of equal strength and thickness. To ascertain whether the vibrations of a string are regular and normal or not, take the ends of it between the thumb and finger of each hand, stretch it as tightly as possible, and set it in vibration with the fourth finger.

---

* If an instrument possesses any value at all, it is always worth while to take it to a good dealer, let him by trials prove what gauge and quality of strings best suit it, and sell you a string-gauge marked with the results. It pays best in the end.—*Translator*.

If it is a "pure," string, the vibrations will assume this form, without extra lines:—

If the vibrations are not regular and uniform, a third line will be seen, thus:—

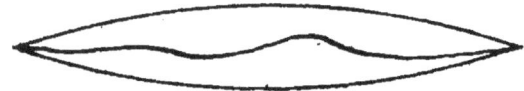

A string is pure in fifths with its neighbouring string, if, when both are pressed down by one finger, they give perfect fifths in all positions. In this regard it should be noted that many strings are thinner at one end than the other. If this gradual thinning goes regularly from one end of the string to the other, its vibrations will be regular and uniform; but, all the same, it will not make pure fifths with the next string in all positions, because, for example, to produce the octave, the string which gradually thins down must not be fingered in the middle but rather nearer to the thicker end. If two strings, say E and A, are each thicker at one end than the other, and the thin portions are at opposite ends (that is, if the thicker end of the A string is at the peg-box and the thicker end of the E string is at the bridge), these two strings cannot possibly make perfect fifths in all positions. The thinner ends of both should be together, and it is better they should be at the bridge end, so as not to impede vibration.

2. THE SOUNDING BODY.

Only the smallest part of the peculiar brilliance of the violin tone comes direct from the strings themselves. To prove this, stretch a string between two pieces of wood, and twang the string, when it will only yield a very thin, faded sort of sound—obviously because there is only the thin surface of the string itself to set the air waves in vibration. To impart power to the tone of the string, a sound-box, or resonance apparatus, is wanted, which is capable of receiving the vibrations from the string and giving them back to the air with much greater force, because coming from a much broader surface than that of the string itself. This sound-box or resonance apparatus (*i.e.*, the body of the violin itself), not only sets in vibration a much larger body of air than the string can possibly do, but also helps to increase the power of tone by the vibrations of the body of air contained within it. Air itself, especially when confined within fixed walls, is so excellent a conductor of sound-producing vibrations, that it materially reinforces the sounding capacity of any body within which it is contained.

The body of the violin, however, not merely increases the volume of the tone of the strings, but has a peculiar effect also upon the quality of the tone; and this fact calls for further discussion.

The tone of the resonance body does not arise from the fact that as a whole it vibrates in unison with the string, or merely as an elastic body, for in that case a scale of equal quality throughout would be an impossibility; that tone depends upon the fact that every minute particle of which that resonance body consists is set in vibratory motion, which motion corresponds in vibration number with that of the string which passes on its vibrations to that body.

The molecules of a sounding body move at every vibratory motion of the string, each in an infinitesimally small space, imparting such motion to each other, and each returning to it former position. The time necessary for these primitive vibrations is quite independent of the vibration of the string, and is conditioned only by the elasticity of the sounding body itself. These two elements—the vibrations of the air and the vibrations of the particles of which the sounding body is composed—fix the tone quality, or "tone colour," of any particular instrument, and, speaking generally, it is thus that we obtain the "woody" tone of a wooden instrument, and the metallic tone of a brass or other instrument made of metal.

We have already learnt that the goodness and usefulness of a string depends upon its elasticity, its weight, and on the necessary uniformity of its shape. These requirements have to be kept in mind in the fashioning of the resonance body. While we have noted that, for instance, the elasticity and the weight of the string must not go beyond a certain limit, we cannot say precisely the same of the resonance body; but it is to be particularly noted that the degree or ratio of each special quality in each of the sounding bodies must stand in the highest possible harmonious relations to each other; for, even with the best stringing attainable, no good violin tone will be possible if the resonance body is handicapped by too much or too little density or thickness.

Thus it follows that the greatest possible care in the selection and working of the materials of the body of the violin becomes of the first and highest importance.

That part of the body which is the most important and most difficult to produce in perfection is the belly. The material most suitable for the required purpose is pine wood.

Steel, glass, and pine possess the first essential, elasticity, in the highest, and in proportion to their weight in an almost equal, degree; and yet the two first-named materials can scarcely be considered in the matter of violin making, if we remember that steel, for example, is fourteen times heavier than pine, and also, further, that if made so thin as not to be too heavy, it would yield a clanking, rattling tone instead of the sweet but powerful tone given out by wood.

A further peculiarity shown by pine wood over all other materials, is its fibrous constitution, by which means it transmits vibrations in a given direction to an extraordinary extent.

Savart measured the elasticity of various woods by the rapidity with which they communicated sound. He found that in pine wood this rapidity in the direction of the grain, was just as great as was the case with hard and solid materials like glass and steel, viz., from fifteen to sixteen and a half times greater than in air, the latter being counted as unity. Transversely to the direction of the grain, he found the rapidity of conveying sound was not nearly so great, being only from two to four times greater than in air, according to whether the grain was broad or narrow, but in no case over five times greater.

Leaving aside the further results which followed Savart's experiments, we pass on to the practical suggestions made by Dr. Schafhäutl as to the selection of wood.

The wood for the belly is obtained from the pine and the fir.

As the scientific names of these forest trees are not by any means definitely settled, it is necessary, if one wishes to quote the names of these trees with needle-shaped leaves, to give at the same time the name of the authors who use those names, so as to avoid the danger of recommending a wood which is something quite different from what is intended.

"By *fir*," says Dr. Schafhäutl, " we mean the *abies pectinata*, so named by Decandolle, and known as silver fir, pitch pine, etc., etc.

By *pine*, we refer to *abies excelsa poir*.

" The wood of the silver fir is usually regarded as in every way the most suitable for instruments. That, however, is not always the case, and I am convinced that for the most and the best instruments pine, and not fir, is used. With respect to the qualities of pine as a sounding wood, it must be observed that not only are its rings at a suitable distance from each other, and most distinctly marked, but these rings are also transversely joined together, as it were, horizontally by those beautiful streaks which extend from the centre of the back, and which are known by the name 'pith rays' or 'pith bands.' By the structure of these peculiar streaks or rays, a special brilliance is imparted to the surface of the wood when split, which the workman call the looking-glass."

In our southern mountains, whence came the wood for Stainer's violins, and to some extent also that used for the Cremonese instruments, grows the pine which makes the most excellent bellies; though even here it is only one of four varieties of pine, all well known to the mountaineers, but which remain quite unknown to the botanists. Of these four varieties of pine, which in the south Bavarian mountains and in the so-called Bavarian forests bordering on Austria and Bohemia, grows the pine which gives the best musical results—the so-called " hazel pine," though this name does not appear in any of the botanical books. The essential marks by which this pine is known are these:—a pale rose-red male flower, and a green female flower; cones which when young are light green, but which when ripe are long and of the colour of rust; and a bright green crown, visible a long way off.

The best hazel pine is that which grows in deep valleys, well protected from winds and storms, and where the soil is rather poor; it must be of sufficient age for the tubes of the woody fibre to have become well filled out and permanent in structure. Stainer always selected his own wood, and would used none but what came from trees the tops of which had already begun to die off.

It is a mistake to maintain, as some do, that the finer and closer the grain of the pine, the better it is suited for violin bellies; and it is equally an error to seek for the desired excellence only in pine of a very broad grain. It may be taken as a rule that the grain should be neither too fine nor too broad: for a very close grain may mean that the tree has been stunted in its development, and a very broad grain may indicate a too rapid and luxuriant growth—and in both cases the growth and development of the tree may not have been normal.

But there are exceptions even to this rule; and while

very excellent instruments are to be met with the belly-wood of which is of a very close grain, others equally excellent are found with broad-grained wood.

Makers have universally agreed that pine is the best belly-wood; but there is not the same unanimity as to the best wood for the back and sides. It is quite true that by far the greater number of instruments made in Italy have backs and sides of maple; but even in Italy this was not always the case. Thus the writer knows a 'cello, said to have been made by Guarnerius del Gesu, which has a back of very soft wood. Among seventeenth century makers of the second and third rank, frequent use was made (for backs and sides) of pine, fir, and lime. Dr. Schebek has in his possession a 'cello, made in 1659, of which the back is of lime and the sides of beech. There are of course various sorts of lime-wood; and I have seen a letter from a great connoisseur of instruments, who owns a G. B. Ruggieri 'cello with a back of Italian lime, in which he expressly states that this is a particularly hard wood.

Modern makers universally use maple for backs and sides, and they prefer wood which has the most "flame" in it, because it increases the beauty of the instruments. But it is now believed that wood without "flame" is best fitted for the production of a good tone.

However pleasant, sweet, and round may be the tone of old instruments made with backs and bellies both of soft wood—and those qualities are especially found when back and belly are cut the same way of the grain—that tone is, all the same, not so powerful, nor does it "carry" so well, as when the back is of maple. The tone at once gains in power when the soft back is taken from an instrument and a maple back put in its place.

This fact proves that the back has a somewhat different function to discharge from that of the belly. Vibration is not the main function of the back, which to a certain extent only echoes, or repeats, the vibration of the belly. If the back vibrates with the same power as the belly, it would seem that its effect would be to

H

disturb the air-waves caused by the vibrations of the belly. We are therefore bound to conclude that the office of the back is to offer a certain resistance to the force of the air-waves caused in the body of contained air by the vibrations of the belly, which resistance, however, must not go beyond a certain point, lest the vibrating power of the back should be destroyed altogether.

The working of the wood for the belly and back must be carried out according to certain fixed rules, which have been evolved from long experience in the art; for however excellent may be the materials used, there is no instrument in which the various parts must be so mathematically proportioned one to the other as that apparently simple instrument the violin. The thicknesses of back and belly are of the utmost possible importance; and a very small variation therein will completely change the character of the instrument. If the wood is too thick, the tone will be poor and without any "ringing" quality; if the wood is too thin, the tone will be hollow and "tubby," as the instrument makers say.

The elasticity of the resonance body is increased by the arching. The higher that arching is, the greater will be its power of resistance, and so much less strength of wood will be wanted; and of course, on the other hand, a lower arching wants more thickness of wood. It is on account of their flatter arching that the violins of Stradivarius are stronger in wood than those of the Amati.

The apportioning of the thicknesses amongst the several parts of the belly is also a matter of the very highest importance. In this respect the greatest masters worked on various principles, just as they did in the matter of the arching; and the right distribution of the thicknesses is also a weighty factor in determining the quality of tone.

The position and form of the so-called "sound-holes" are of very great importance. The sound-holes show how even the most famous acousticians have, in their experiments and attempts, neglected entirely the very essentials of the art of violin making. Most of them have regarded the sound-holes as mere openings to let out the tone from the body of air vibrating within the instrument. But no sooner do we place these "mere openings" in another position, or alter their form, than we cause the instrument to lose the greater part of its special violin tone. The famous Savart, when he made his four-cornered "fiddle" with flat back and belly, with two straight slits for the sound-holes, had merely in view two vibrating flat slabs of wood, one of which transmitted its vibrations to the other by means of a simple wooden post.

Antonio Bagatella, in 1782, won a prize from the University of Padua for his rules for producing, with the greatest geometrical precision, the various parts of the violin, down to the smallest and apparently most insignificant member. These rules were the result of thirty years' work and experience, and they are as follows:—

"Draw a line as long as the violin is to be,* and divide this line into seventy-two exactly equal parts. This is the foundation of the entire work. The lines marking off these seventy-two parts must be drawn with the utmost exactitude, for upon this everything depends. This vertical line divides the belly into two exactly equal halves. (See Fig. 18). Through this line draw seven other lines at right angles with it, with all possible care and precision. Draw the first line through point 14, the second through point 20, the third through point 25, and the others through points 33, 43, 48, and 57. Then put one leg of the compasses on the point X, measure off nine points, and from the centre X describe the two small arcs A and B. Then take the point 24 as a centre, open the compasses to the point X, and describe the arc A X B. Cut off, from the horizontal line through point 14, two parts C, C; take each of these as a centre, and,

---

* This means of course the *body* of the violin, and not the entire length from the scroll.—*Translator*

opening the compasses on the one side to A, and on the other side to B, draw the two arcs A D and B D, so that each arc shall reach the horizontal line through point 20. Thus we have the upper part of the instrument.

"When this has been done, mark on the horizontal line through point 33 two points E E, each ten and a half parts* from point 33; and from these both points F F, which then become the centres of the two semicircles H, E, G, so that in this manner we get the outline of the middle part of the instrument.

"Now, from the point 72, open the compasses nine parts, and describe the two little arcs I, K; then, on the horizontal line through point 57, mark three parts towards L L, and likewise three parts towards M M; take these as centres, and at the distance on the one side of M K, and at the distance on the other side of M J, make the arcs N K and N J. Take the point L as a centre, open the compasses to N, and make on each side the arc N O. Finally, place one leg of the compasses at point 72, and make the arc K Y J. Then the entire outline is completed, and this figure, drawn on wood of suitable thickness, gives the model of the instrument."

Bagatella goes on to say that the upper quoins must be ten parts broad and four parts thick; the lower quoins of the same thickness, but only eight parts broad. The four corner quoins must fall between points 20 to 25, and 43 to 48. The height of the sides, where they meet at the tail-piece button, must be $6\frac{1}{4}$ parts, narrowing down to 6 parts at the point where the neck fits in.

It is a curious fact that Bagatella insists on the back being of more importance than the belly; whereas all instrument makers, in studying the patterns left by the greatest masters, lay greatest stress upon the belly,—so much so, that by the belly the authenticity of the instrument can be completely established, even though every other part is quite new and modern.

---

* That is, ten and a half of the seventy-two parts into which the vertical line is divided. The drawing at the right hand side of Fig. 18 shows the amount of arching of belly and back.—*Translator*.

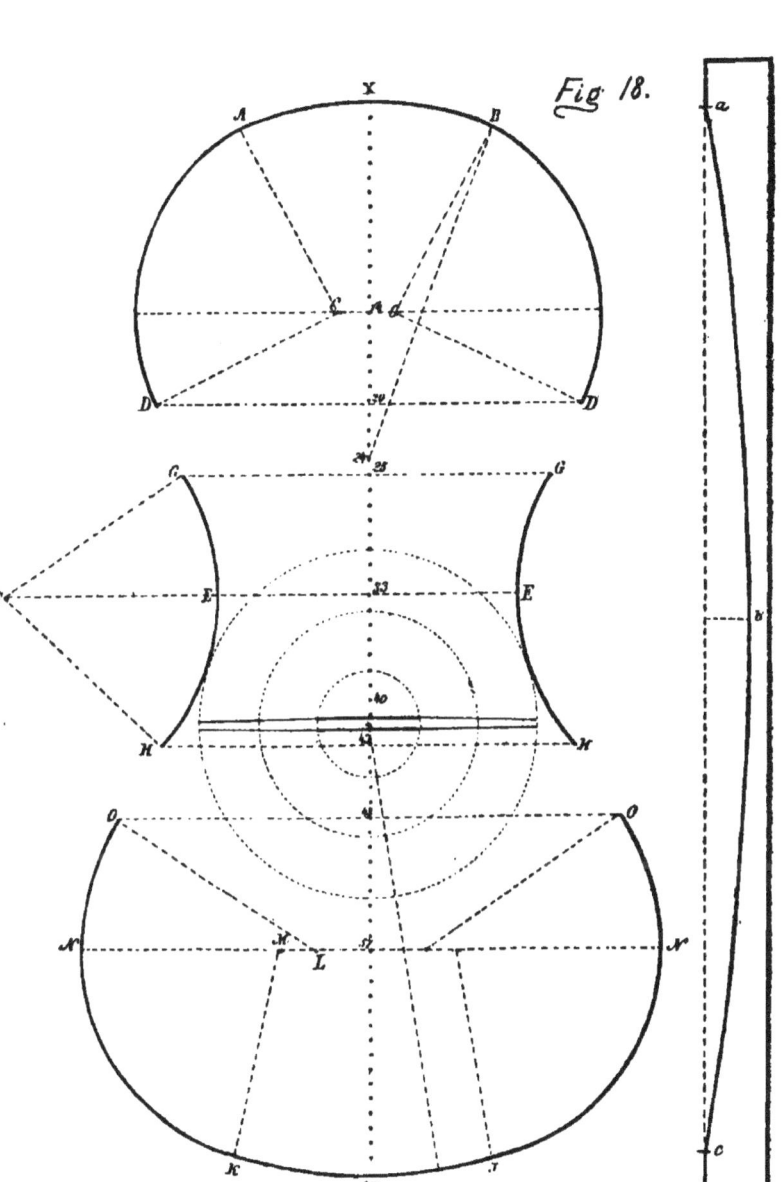

Fig. 18.

But if the violin maker wishes to work neither on Bagatella's model nor yet upon one of his own, he can still—and this is by far the best course—take an established pattern, so long as he is careful to assure himself that his pattern is genuine, and has not been "tinkered" or tampered with. In our day the model of Stradivarius is the one which, with proper care in following it, yields by far the best results.

We must here say, yet once more, that the selection of good wood is, and remains, of the very greatest importance. Without this, all patterns and all rules are useless, and the most skilful and careful worker cannot attain to excellence without an intimate knowledge of the materials upon which he works. Our greatest masters are known not merely by the exterior splendour of their instruments, but more than all by their intimate knowledge of their wood; and they never wasted their art upon inferior materials. The instruments of the Italian makers were eagerly sought, and well paid for. Thus they achieved a prosperous position, and could well afford to use only the very best materials. On this point a well-known author says:—

"Vuillaume journeyed almost every year to Switzerland and the Tyrol in search of the best wood. Wherever he found a door, a table, or a bench likely to serve his purpose, he straightway bought it; and by means of hard cash, despoiled the instrument makers and timber dealers of their best stuff. Who then amongst our own people, or amongst existing Italian makers, is able to do as Vuillaume does, enjoying as he does an assured independent annual income of £1,200 a year? What avails if our makers copy the great masters? The secret lies not in the outward shape. I have seen so many imitations, made with wondrous skill, but at the finish I can only say—Stradivarius would never have touched these materials. The copyist cuts everything in strict accordance with all the rules; but his copy is still *only* a copy."

3. The Bass Bar, Sound Post, and Bridge.

These parts are absolutely indispensable, as without them the best instrument will give but a very poor tone; yet these parts will not turn a badly made fiddle into a good one. They are, moreover, in these days, as well made and as carefully finished, by every thoughtful and experienced violin maker, as those to be found in the best Cremonese instruments, and there are but few of those instruments left in which this or that detail has not been replaced by a new one, and probably not one single Cremona fiddle can be found in which every detail is left as it came from the maker's hands. The parts now under consideration have been renewed by repairers in so skilful a manner that it is almost impossible to say that the instrument has suffered by the change.

The removal of the bass-bar from old instruments, however well they were originally made, and however carefully they have been preserved, has in the lapse of time become a necessity, because the old masters left this part too weak. This is especially the case with Stradivarius and Guarnerius. Yet the reader must not for a moment imagine that these masters made a mistake, or that they underestimated the importance of the bass-bar; for, in their instruments, that important feature was adapted with the utmost nicety and care to the pitch, and consequent pressure of the strings on the belly, which prevailed in their own day. Tartini estimated, in 1734, that the pressure of the strings on the belly was equal to a weight of sixty-three pounds; and we can only infer from this estimate that the strings used by Tartini must have been thinner than those now in use, and that on account of the lesser height of his bridge, the strings made a less acute angle at the bridge than is now the case. Since Tartini's day the pitch has notably risen, and the height of the bridge has been increased; the pressure of the strings on the belly has become proportionately greater, rendering it necessary to strengthen the bass-bar, so as to enable the belly to resist the greater pressure it is called on to bear.

Vuillaume believed that the "enormous pressure" of the strings on the belly would gradually bring about the entire destruction of all the old instruments.

The proper position for the bass-bar is such that the left foot of the bridge stands right over it. Its purpose is to bear the weight on that side, and it follows that it must be so adjusted, and be made of such a strength as to bear its burden without sinking.

The opinions of even the best makers are at variance on this point; and as the thickness of the belly has to be kept strictly in view in making the bass-bar, it is very difficult, if not quite impossible, to give any fixed rules as to its size and proportions. The higher or lower arching of any particular instrument will also have a definite effect in determining the length of the bass-bar. Some think they have discovered the philosopher's stone by fixing the bar "on the straight;" others "find salvation" in putting it a bit "on the slant;" while others regard the point as of no importance. An artist once asked Stoss, of Vienna, about the position of the bass-bar, and he said, "If the wood and the workmanship are all right, you can put the bass-bar where you like—it would still be a good fiddle." To another, who asked him how he placed it, he said, "I don't know—I put it just where it seems to me best." To a third he said, "Drop all speculation about the bass-bar. If you can invent a machine by which we can lengthen or shorten the sound-post by a hair's breadth where it stands, *and without taking it out of the fiddle*, we have learned the great secret—we want nothing else."*

The other foot of the bridge—that on the E string side—also wants support, and this is furnished by a vertical and cylindrical post, standing firmly between belly and back. This post must not, however, stand

---

* Stoss's remarks come to this:—A good maker wants knowledge, experience, and, above all, *intuition*.—*Translator*.

exactly under the foot of the bridge, as in that case the vibrations of the bridge would for the most part be transmitted directly to the back, and the tone would be dull and stifled; it must be put *behind* the bridge foot (nearer the tail piece) about 6mm. The essential point in placing the sound-post is that it is precisely of the right length, and that it shall be neither too tightly nor too loosely fixed between the two tables. The French, with great truth, call the sound-post "the soul" (l'âme) of the violin.

Spohr gaves the following directions for the placing of the sound-post:—

"Before any experimenting can be done with the bridge, the sound-post must be set up. For this a sound-post setter is used (see Fig. 25*). Fix the point of the setter about half an inch from the end which is to support the belly, and then pass it through the right sound-hole into the inside of the violin, press the lower end firmly on the back, and draw out the setter till the top of the post rests against the belly.

"Now reverse the setter, and draw the post forward with the hook, or push it back with the semicircle, till it is in its proper place. This is usually close behind the bridge's right foot, so that the fore edge of the post may be in a line with the back part of the bridge foot. The sound-post must stand perfectly upright, and the ends should be worked with a fine file till they fit belly and back with the greatest exactness. This is a hard task, and can only be properly done by looking into the inside of the fiddle through the hole into which the tail-piece button fits. The upper edge of the post must be rounded off a bit, so that when moved about it will not press into the soft belly-wood.

"Whether the upper end of the sound-post is in its proper place can only be known by measuring with a piece of fine wire, hooked so as to go through the sound-hole, and then holding the wire over the belly to see if

---

* See Folding Plate.

the distance is right. If it is, bring the lower end of the post to its proper position, so that the post is upright; this can be known by looking through the sound-hole and the tail-piece button hole.

"The sound-post should not be so long as to raise the belly, nor so short as to fall down, or even be moved, when a string breaks, or from any other shock. When the strings are off, the post should only slightly touch, and be capable of being easily moved to and fro; it should, also, be so placed that its grain is crossways to the grain of the belly, so that it will not press into the belly. Whether the post should be large or small, of wide or close grain, can be only settled by experiments; but, generally speaking, a thick belly will want a thicker sound-post than one which is weak in wood.

"When these directions have been carried out, if the violin does not sound freely, or is unequal in tone, move the post backwards and forwards until you have found, by repeated trials, that the instrument gives the most sonorous and powerful tone it is capable of producing, and until the tone of all four strings is equal. If the tone is equal, but rough and hard, move the post a little back from the foot of the bridge; if the upper strings sound shrill, and the lower ones weak, move the post nearer to the bass-bar; but if the lower strings on the contrary are harsh and the upper ones feeble, move the post towards the sound-hole."

The object of the *Bridge* is to convey to the belly the vibrations of the strings which cross it. Its shape, which at first sight would appear to be the outcome of mere whim or caprice, cannot be changed in the most minute degree without damage to the tone of the instrument. If, for instance, the bridge is shaped as a mere thin plate of wood, of the same external form as the proper bridge, the violin will give out hardly any tone at all; if a space is cut out so as to give the bridge its two feet, the tone increases in power; and as one detail after another is cut out, it will be found that the nearer the shape of this dummy bridge gets to the form of the

THE VIOLIN AND ITS STORY. 107

prototype, the more will the tone develop in power. Numerous attempts have been made to find out when this most important, though apparently not important, part of the violin was brought to its present state of perfection. Leaving out of the question the endless examples of different forms of bridge which are found on monuments and in old books, Vuillaume's information on this subject is of great interest. Fig. 19 belonged to a seven-stringed

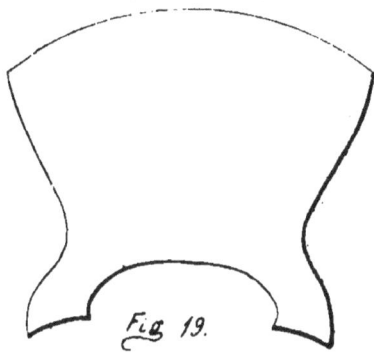

viol, and is only cut at the two sides; Fig. 20, which has

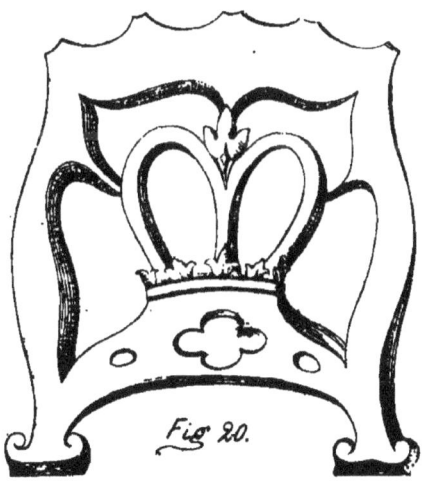

much more cut away, is from a five-stringed viol; Fig. 21

is the bridge of a small sized violin from the old school of Anton Amati; and Fig. 22 was on a violin of

Nicholas Amati. The last two are almost of the form of the present bridge, but show some differences in respect to the number and direction of the cuts. It was the bridge of Stradivarius (Fig. 23) which fixed the form of that article for all time.

The attempts to fit a bridge to a violin must be carried out with great industry, and still greater attention and patience; and these attempts can only be begun after the sound-post has been brought to its proper position. The mutual adjustment of the sound-post and bridge should be a matter with which the violin player is thoroughly familiar, because, as before stated, it has a most intimate connection with the tone of the instrument. Instrument makers, as a rule, do not devote sufficient trouble to this

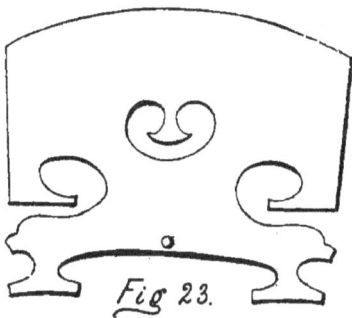

essential matter unless they are familiar with the particular fiddle they have in hand, or else, on the other hand, they are not good players, and have not a sufficiently delicate and artistic ear to differentiate between one shade of tone and another.

The bridge is made of " stippled " maple, and its height, width, strength, and weight must be most accurately adjusted to the condition and constitution of the violin itself. The proportions of the height and strength (or thickness) of the bridge cannot be determined by any fixed rules, because instruments are so varied in make and in the details of their construction, and cannot on that account be all treated alike. As a general rule, however, the height of the bridge should not go beyond two-thirds of the length of the sound-post. Fiddles with a high arching, like those of the Stainer model, usually require a higher bridge. But the height is generally of less moment than the weight, because the height must of necessity be regulated more or less by the position of the fingerboard. The thickness of the bridge, on the contrary, on which its *weight* depends, has a most important effect on the vibrating capacity of the bridge, and, in consequence, on the tone itself. The bridge is the medium by which the vibrations of the strings are communicated to the body of the violin. Thus, if the bridge is too strong in weight, it is more difficult to set it in vibration, and has a correspondingly less effect upon the belly; if, on the other hand, it is too light, there is a similar defect in the other direction.

The following is the best way to fit a proper bridge which shall satisfy all the requirements of the instrument:—Prepare a number of bridges of varying weight, some strong and some weak in wood, some of soft and some of hard wood, but all of them made of the oldest and most seasoned material to be obtained, and all finished alike, *as to width*, so as to meet in this respect the special needs of the particular instrument. This question of width can only be determined by placing the left foot of the bridge exactly over the middle of the bass-bar. When this condition is fulfilled, and the two feet of the bridge are at exactly equal distances from the sound-holes, the right *width* of the bridge has been found. Then finish off all the bridges at the right height. This depends, as above stated, on the position of the finger-board and the arching of the violin. The arch of the bridge should be as shown in Fig. 24 (below). Next see that the feet of your collection of bridges are all so shaped as to exactly fit the curve of the belly. Then you can begin trying your bridges one by one till you find *the* one which brings out the best tone; and in this connection it must be noted that the feet of your bridge must be exactly in a line with the small cuts in the sound-holes.

In order that the ear may be able to discern the slight differences of tone produced by the different bridges, the changes must be made as quickly as possible. In order to effect these changes without slackening the strings, when you have tried one bridge, put in one half an inch nearer the fingerboard, keeping this one at hand and using it for the same purpose all through. This auxiliary bridge will tighten the strings so that you can take out the bridge you have tried, and put in the next for trial, in a few seconds. Only, be very careful that the sharp edges of the feet of your bridges make no marks on the varnish of the belly.

THE NECK

is also made of maple. This is fixed with glue only, and not with nails or screws.

The best wood for the fingerboard is ebony. No softer wood will resist the constant pressure of the strings by the fingers, and any other wood will soon show those indentations which are such a nuisance to the player. The fingerboard is rounded somewhat similar to the top of the bridge, but with a somewhat flatter arch.

Spohr, in his "Violin School," refers to a slight hollowing out of the fingerboard under the G string as follows:—"On the fingerboard of my violin is the hollowing out underneath the G string (shown in the following figure), which grows gradually smaller towards the nut. The advantage of this is that it gives more

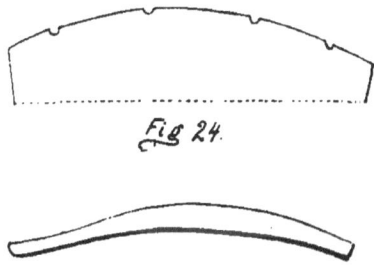

Fig 24.

space for the vibrations of the string, and prevents that disagreeable jarring so often heard with a strong pressure of the bow. This hollowing-out is the invention of Bernhard Romberg, who had it made under the C string of his violoncello. I tried it on my violin twenty-five years ago,* and it has proved of great utility."

The *Nut*, or saddle, must be only very slightly raised

---

* The preface to the "Violin School" is dated "Cassel, March, 1832."—*Translator.*

above the fingerboard, and so "nicked" that more room is left for the free vibrations of the G and D strings than for the A and E.

THE BOW.*

Like the violin itself, the bow has passed through its own stages of development. As bowed instruments have improved, so also has the bow itself been brought ever nearer to perfection. The improvements in the bow, however, reached their highest point a century later than the violin was perfected; and both violin and bow have reached the point beyond which no further betterment is possible.

In its original form, the bow with which the Rebek was played, greatly resembled its namesake used in battle. The stick was very much bent, and a string or piece of gut was tied to each end. In the thirteenth century the germs of a nut and of a head began to appear; and this favours the presumption that, even thus early, the bow was made with hair stretched from end to end; and also, that the stick had become much less curved than was previously the case. In the third phase of its development, the bow assumed a still less curved form; the head has become well developed, while the nut is no longer cut from the same piece of wood as the bow itself, but has become a distinct member by itself, which is secured to the stick by wire, and on the back of the stick are pieces of toothed metal to which this wire can be fastened so as to obtain the required tension on the hair. Such a bow was used by Corelli (1653-1713) and by Vivaldi (died 1743). These two masters, who flourished at the end of the seventeenth and the beginning of the eighteenth centuries, did not feel the necessity for a bow with a flexible stick, because the style of their play, corres-

---

* Abele's work gives the excellent series of sketches included in Fig. 26, but makes no reference to them in his text. He probably assumes that the intelligence of his readers will understand that the drawings represent the development of the bow from 1620 to 1790.—*Translator*.

Fig. 26.

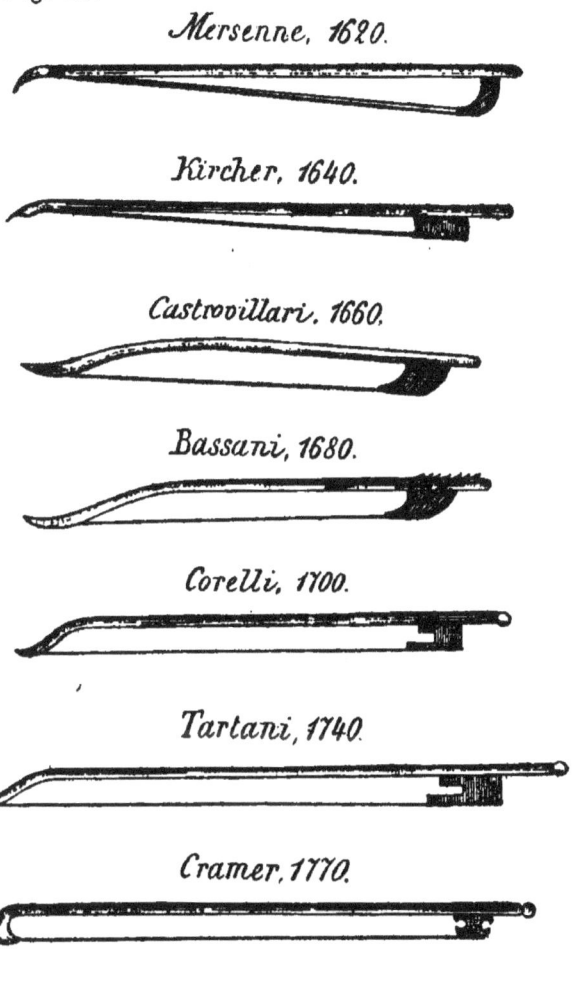

The Evolution of the Bow.

ponding with the taste of the period, did not call for delicate and manifold shades of tone-colour exhibited in later compositions, and for which special qualities in the bow became an absolute necessity. Corelli and Vivaldi knew but one style of play, to which their bow was adapted, viz., to play a movement over *piano*, and then repeat it *forte*.*

In the fourth stage of development, the wire and the toothed iron were succeeded by a screw in the stick, and through an opening on the under side of the stick passed a female screw fixed to the nut, so that the necessary tension of the bow-hair could be adjusted with the greatest nicety. This construction is found in the bow used by Tartini (died 1770), the famous composer of the "Devil's Sonata," whose style was much more varied than that of either Corelli or Vivaldi. Tartini had his bow made of light wood, and with the stick straight, instead of being bent as it was before his time. His bow had a shorter head, and the part of the stick held by the hand in playing was grooved. This style of bow was, however, not free from defects, and many attempts were made to get better materials and improve the shape. But the man who brought the bow to its highest pitch of development was François Tourte, who was born in Paris in 1774, and died in April, 1835. Tourte's father before him was a skilled workman in this department. He made fluted bows of splendid workmanship, and cut deeper into the head, so that the hair could be more easily fixed, and the hairs laid side by side with greater regularity. The bows of his eldest son, who began to manufacture about 1775, were also greatly prized.

François Tourte was intended by his father for a watch maker, and was placed in a workshop at a very early age, when he could neither read nor write. Probably it was from this kind of work that he got the skill

---

* The student who knows Corelli's works will understand this. Those compositions were essentially for the left hand, the bow being in Corelli's day merely the "tool" with which the notes made by the left hand were made audible.—*Translator*.

of finger and delicacy of touch that were of such value to him as a maker of bows. When he had worked at the watch making for eight years he left it, because it offered him no prospects, and went to work at the business of his father and brother. The violin virtuosi who at that time lived in Paris, who were ever striving to imitate the style of the Italian vocalists in all their delicate variations of tone, sought more and more eagerly for bows of greater lightness, buoyancy and elasticity, and the bow-makers were as eagerly trying to satisfy these requirements. François Tourte made his earliest bows with wood obtained from sugar-barrels, and thus trained his hand without spoiling valuable wood. His first productions sold at about 10d. to 1s. 3d. each. Unwearying in his efforts to accomplish his purpose, he made bows of every kind of wood which was at all suitable for the purpose; and he was a long time in arriving at the firm conviction that it was only from Brazil wood that the proper results could be got which would unite in themselves the requisite qualities of lightness, firmness and elasticity.

These first and important discoveries were made by Tourte in the period between 1775 and 1780. Unfortunately at this time the naval war between France and England made it very difficult to import Brazil wood, and that of the right kind for dyeing purposes rose to between 5s. and 6s. per pound. This wood, when used for dyeing, was imported in logs or billets, and that wood which contained the most dye-stuff was at the same time the best fitted to make bows. It was, moreover, only seldom that a log could be found perfectly even and free from knots, and out of 8,000 to 10,000 kilograms* of wood scarcely one good stick could be found.

The great scarcity of Brazil wood during the period above referred to explains the high prices at which Tourte sold his best bows. One bow, the nut of which was ornamented with tortoise-shell and the head with mother-of-pearl, both nut and head having gold orna-

---

* 10,000 kilograms = 22,046 lbs. English weight.—*Translator.*

ments, sold for ten guineas; his best bows, ornamented with silver, and with ebony nut, sold at £3; and his ordinary bows, without ornament of any kind, sold at thirty shillings.

Up to 1775, neither the length and weight of a bow, nor the conditions of its balance in the hand, were in any way fixed. With the advice of the famous artists with whom he conferred, Tourte fixed the length of the violin bow (including the head) at 74 or 75 centimetres; the viola bow at 74; and the 'cello bow at 72 to 73.* At the same time, also, he decided the distance of the hair from the stick by the size of the head and nut. By these proportions he also pitched on the necessary angle at which the hair should be to properly grip the strings, and got rid of the disadvantage arising from the hair coming into contact with the stick. As his bows had a higher head, and therefore a heavier head, than those of his predecessors, he increased in a marked degree the weight of the lower end of the bow, so that the point of greatest weight was brought close to the hand, and the essential balance preserved. With this object he freely loaded the tip and the head with metal ornaments, in order to increase their weight.

Vuillaume, to whom we are indebted for this account of Tourte, himself saw how Tourte sawed up his blocks of Brazil wood so as to get the right grain, and how he got the right curves by heating the wood. Some few maintained that Tourte did not bend his sticks by means of heat, but that he sawed them out of the required form. But this idea is directly contradicted by the fact that the fibre of the wood runs right through the bent stick, the advantages of which Tourte soon recognised. He also made it a principle that the wood must be heated all through alike, the centre as well as the outside.

---

* 72 centimetres = 28·347 inches.
  73 ,,   = 28.741 ,,
  74 ,,   = 29,134 ,,
  75 ,,   = 29,328 ,,
                               —*Translator*.

When Viotti came to Paris, in 1786, it was usual to put on the hair in a round bunch or sheaf, which hindered the production of a good quality of tone. Tourte changed this by fixing his hair in the form of a broad band or ribbon.

The excellence of Tourte's bows lies in three points:— (1) their lightness, owing to the adequate elasticity of the wood; (2) their beautifully equal curve, which brings to the middle of the stick the spot where the hair is nearest to it; and (3) their extraordinarily exact and neat workmanship. The perfection of Tourte's fabrications has never since been reached; and hence it is, that while his bows now fetch from £8 to £12, the best bows of present day makers can be bought for £1 to £1 5s.*

Next to Tourte's bows, those of Lafleur, of Paris, and Schwartz, of Strasburg, are in the greatest demand; and, in our own time, J. Henry and P. Simon, both of Paris, have attained celebrity as bow-makers.

It was not splendid workmanship alone which made Tourte's bows famous, but the fact that he possessed the most perfect insight and knowledge of the nature of the materials he used, which has never been equalled by anyone either before or since his time.

Many attempts have been made to manufacture bows with other woods, but the special qualities of weight, firmness, tenacity, and elasticity are found nowhere else so fittingly blended as in Brazil wood.

It is not without reason that for double-bass bows black hair is used instead of white. The tail hair of the male horse is strongest and most durable, and especially is this the case with black hair. The hairs of the mare are finer and less durable in use, but they are also more greasy and unequal, and therefore are not used for the very best bows.

If a single horse hair be drawn through the fingers

---

* Abele of course had never heard of our great modern bow makers. A fine modern bow by one of the finest bow makers sells easily from £5 to £10.—*Translator.*

from its root to its point, it will offer hardly any resistance; but if it is drawn in the opposite direction considerable roughness will be felt. Under the microscope the reason of this is apparent, for each hair is seen to have a number of minute horny bristles, or cuticles, which all point away from the root of the hair. In arranging the hairs for the bow, they are laid alternately in opposite directions, so that whether the bow goes up or down there shall be an equal number of these cuticles in operation. It is beyond all question that it is these cuticles which cause the "bite" of the hair on the string. When these cuticles are all, or nearly all, worn off by use, no amount of resin will give the hair the necessary "bite"; the hair is then, as we say, "played out."

The number of hairs in a bow was formerly, in France, from 80 to 100; but now-a-days the hair ribbon is broader, and contains from 175 to 250 single hairs.

The hairs must be at least twenty-six inches long. Tourte bestowed extraordinary care in the selection of hair for his bows. He preferred French horse-hair, because it was stronger than that brought in in the way of trade with other countries. He first washed it with soap and water, to free it from grease, and then washed and re-washed it in other ways to get rid of all foreign matters. His daughter was continuously employed in the selection of hair, so as to throw out those which were too short, or were not perfectly cylindrical; for, taking the hairs as they come to hand, there is only about one in ten which is of any use for bow-making, as most of them present a flat surface, and are full of inequalities. It will, of course, be easily understood that in arranging the hairs, they must be stretched as nearly alike as possible, must lie in an even row side by side, and that none of the hairs must cross. New hair does not grip well, and produces a rough tone. A new bow must be used three or four weeks before it is fit for solo playing. After use the bow should be unscrewed, so that the elasticity of the stick is not impaired.

In conclusion, I will briefly offer a few general observations.

Though a violin be made with the greatest care and by the greatest master, and of the finest materials, it will at first be somewhat rough in tone, and somewhat slow of "speech." In order to lose these undesirable qualities, a violin must be played, and *well* played, year in and year out. It is believed that a violin does not reach its full power and its best condition until it has been made and played from thirty to forty years.

He who possesses a good violin should see to it that for the repairing of those defects which will insinuate themselves into the best instruments, only a thoroughly good and well-known repairer should be consulted. Good repairers, it is true, are very scarce, but their fame is so wide-spread that there is no difficulty in finding them. An instrument, however, can be well preserved by its owner if he will but bestow sufficient pains and attention on the care of it. The violin should be kept in an easy fitting, thickly made, and tightly closing case, and when cased should be covered by a silken covering to protect it from the effects of the external air, and kept in a dry and moderately warm situation. It should never be left long out of its case, and never taken out of the house unless it is carefully shut up in its cosy bed. After use, always clean the instrument with a soft, dry cloth, to clear off all resin, dust, or other foreign matters before closing it up, especially from the belly, strings and fingerboard; otherwise the vibrations will be hindered and moisture will be attracted.

THE END.

INDEX.

A

	PAGE
Agricola's "Musica Instrumentalis"..	23
Albani, M...	59
,, Paul..	59
Albinus, 4-stringed Viol	17
Amati, Andreas	38
,, Hieronymus	40
,, Antonius	40
,, Nicholas	41

B

Back and Belly, functions of	97
Bagatella's Model ..	101
Bagatella's Rules ..	99
Balthazarini (1570)..	33
Barrington, Daines, on the 6-stringed Crouth	9
Bass-bar	103
Bergonzi, M. A. ..	51
,, C. ..	51
Bow, The ..	112
,, Evolution of ..	113
,, nothing like it in Greek and Roman Sculpture ..	3
Bowed Instruments, ancient	14
Brescia, School of ..	36
Bridges, Models of, 107, 108, 109	
Bridge ..	106
,, curve of	111

C

Care of the Violin ..	118
'Cello Bow, length of	116
Combination Tones	83
Corelli's Bow	113
Copying ..	75
Cramer's Bow	113
Cremonese Fiddles, imitation of ..	74
Crouth or Crowth ..	7
,, a Welsh instrument	7
,, 3-stringed ..	7, 8
,, 6 ,,	9
,, ,, tuning of..	10

D

Dardelli, Pietro (1500)	35
Decline of the Art of Violin making ..	72

	PAGE
Doni, J. B., on the "Mágadis"	2
Duiffoprugar, Kaspar (1510)	35

F

Fétis on the Ravanastron ..	3
,, on 6-stringed Crouth..	9
,, Virdung's "great fiddle"	22
"Fiddles" mentioned in 1228	19
Fiddle, great..	21, 22
,, little ..	24
Finger-board, Spohr on	111
French makers	63
Frets, use of..	25

G

Gagliano	55
German School	55
Great Fiddle..	21, 22
,, ,, tuning of	25
Greek Mágadi	2
Greeks & Romans, stringed instruments of	2
Guadagnini, L.	51
Guarnerius, Andreas	48
,, del Jesu	97
,, Joseph..	48, 49
,, J. A. ..	48
,, Peter ..	48
Guilds of Musicians	20

H

Hans Judenkünig ..	26, 27
Harmonics ..	83
Horse-hair for Bows	117

I

India, cradle of stringed instruments ..	3

J

Judenkünig ..	26, 27

K

Kerlino, Johann (1449)	
Klotz, Egidius	
,, Matthäus ..	60

L

Landolphi ..	51
Little Fiddle	24
Linarolli (1520)	36
Lirone	2
Lupot, Nicholas	63

INDEX—*continued*.

M

Mágadis	2
Maggini, J. P. (1590)	37
,, S.	38
Marini, A. (1570)	38
Markneukirchen	66
Mersenne on Strings	82
Minnesingers	19
Milanese makers	51
Mirmont, of Paris	66
Mirecourt Factories	65
Mittenwald	60
Morelli, M. (1540)	36

N

Naples makers	55
Neapolitan String manufacture	87
Neck	111
Notker's Psalm Book	12
Nut	111

O

Omerti	5
Orchestra first formed	19

P

Paduan firsts are the best	91
Paganini's Guarnerius	51
Pith rays in belly pine	96
Plectrum	3
Prætorius's "Syntagma Musica," 1619	29
"Prison Josephs"	50

R

Ravanastron	3, 4
Rebab or Rebek	5, 6, 13
Resonance body	86, 92
Roman stringed instruments	2
Roman makers	54
Ruggieri, F.	51
Ruggerius, J. B.	54

S

Salo, Gaspardi (1613)	36
Savart's experiments	67
Schafhäutl on selection of wood	95
School of Brescia	36
Sound-post	103
,, Spohr on	103
Sounding body	92
Spohr on the Sound-post	103
Spohr's Lupot	64
Storioni	51
Stoss, of Vienna	61
Strings, facts about	79
Strings, acoustic facts about	85
,, how to test	92
,, Spohr on selection of	91
,, pressure on belly	104
Stainer, Jacob	56
Stradivarius	43, 45

T

Tarisio	46, 54
Tartini's Bow	113
Tartini Tones	83
Tenor Gamba	30
Testore	51
Thicknesses of wood	98
Tourte's Bows	114
Troubadours	17

V

Venans Fortunat on the Crouth	7
Venetian makers	52
Vibrations of Strings	86
Viola di Bordune	2
Viol, 4-stringed, tuning of	17
Viola Bow, length of	116
Virdung's Great and Little Fiddle	21, 24
Viol Bastarda	30
Viol di Gamba	30
Viole de Braccio	30
Violin, name came from Italy	31
,, Forerunners of	32
,, used in score of Monteverde's "Orfeo"	33
,, Bow, length of	116
Virdung's "Musika getutscht" (1511)	21
Viotti's Bow	113
Vogler, Abbe, and Combination Tones	84
Vuillaume;	43, 46, 47, 63, 64, 66

Z

Zanetta, P. (1540)	36

www.ingramcontent.com/pod-product-compliance
Lightning Source LLC
Chambersburg PA
CBHW031317150426
43191CB00005B/262